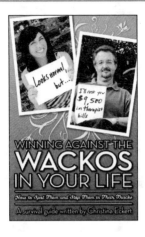

Published by Larstan Publishing, Inc.
10604 Outpost Dr., N. Potomac MD, 20878, 240-396-0007, ext. 901, larstan.com

PRINTED IN THE UNITED STATES OF AMERICA

10 9 8 7 6 5 4 3 2 1

Design by Mike Gibson for the Love Has No Logic Design Group lovehasnologic.com

ISBN, Print Edition 978-0-9776895-8-3

Library of Congress Control Number: 2006938964

First Edition

This book was written as a kind of autobiography of the author's life. The information contained in this book is derived solely on the author's personal observations using fictitious names and sometimes settings. The Authors and Publisher specifically disclaim any responsibility for the likeness of any named character in this book with any like named individual in real life.

WINNING AGAINST THE
WACKOS
IN YOUR LIFE

How To Spot Them and Stop Them in Their Tracks

A survival guide written by Christina Eckert

Every minute of every day, thousands of Wackos are born all over the world.

Dedication

This book is dedicated to the only guy I know who polishes his wedding ring: my husband, Ched. It is also dedicated to all of my best friends: I never cherished you more than after my last Wacko encounter. And to the last Wacko in my life: your behavior inspired me to write this book.

When I embarked upon finding an editor for this project, I felt precisely like "Jerry McGuire" did when he was forced to venture out on his own. I needed that one editor—just one—to see the promise in my work and give this project a chance to get off the ground. I got lucky. I found two! My editors Wendy Cornett and Sue Mellen of YourWriters so believed in my book that they made personal sacrifices for me in order to "Get the job done." With my guard down and my heart open I declare, "Wen and Sue, I adore you both."

And to Dr. Michael Leff: Thank you for saving my life.

Table of Contents

Introduction

This will be my last Wacko experience, I said to myself in a state of pathetic self-loathing. The declaration felt liberating. So I repeated it aloud and with greater conviction: "This *will* be my last Wacko experience."

The collapse of my business partnership wasn't just the last straw; it was the psychological equivalent of getting whacked in the head with a two-by-four. I vowed to live my life differently from that point on and to surround myself with different people.

The label "Wacko" came to me one day while I was trying to make sense of my failed partnership. I had suspected that "Maureen," my former business partner, was unbalanced the very day I met her. But let's face facts; "unbalanced" just doesn't have the same ring to it.

I had known Maureen for more than two years; our daughters were close friends. I watched how Maureen treated people and how she was treated in return. Her relationships were *always* tumultuous. She was insecure, and she habitually belittled and condemned others. She begged me to get into business with her, and I knew better. So, what did I do? I grabbed the opportunity like it was an ice-cold Boodles Gin martini with two large Santa Barbara olives. Our relationship ended exactly as I had witnessed all of her other relationships ending: in a disaster.

Why couldn't I have said "no" to Maureen's business proposition? Why did I think that her relationship with me would somehow be different from her other relationships? Why had I allowed her enthusiasm to blind me to the negative traits I knew she possessed? And, most importantly, did I voluntarily walk into this partnership because I was just that naïve or because she was just that manipulative? These questions gnawed away at my psyche day and night. I consider myself an intelligent person; I knew there had to be a nuts-and-bolts explanation for my lapse in judgment. My self-exploration and discussions with friends and family revealed a pattern: some people are natural parasites and others are natural hosts. The challenge facing the hosts is finding the courage to give personal parasites the big heave-ho for once and for all. Having a "host" personality myself, I have a huge tendency to attract people who exist by draining the souls of others. That's right, dear reader; Maureen was not my first Wacko encounter. But I vowed that Maureen would be the last parasite in my life, and I've kept that promise to myself. While licking my wounds and discussing my self-inflicted business catastrophe with my trustworthy friends and my husband, Ched (who told me *not* to do it in the first place), we all came to the same conclusion: I needed to write a book about Wackos and explore the impact they have on our lives. My pals assured me that everyone has encounters with Wackos and needs the tools for spotting the red flags and cutting his or her losses.

In this book, I describe how to identify the Wackos in your life (some of them can be pretty subversive) and how to protect yourself from them. This book tends to be heavy on female examples, simply because I drew from many of my personal experiences and from those of friends and family. In no way are men immune to hosting and perpetuating Wackodom. In fact, a businessman I recently lunched with begged me for a copy of the unpublished manuscript.

I've created a hierarchy of Wacko levels, ranging from the relatively benign to the soul-sucking, highest levels of parasites. The minute I sat down to write this book, it were as if I were having an out-of-body experience; my fingers typed on autopilot and the words streamed effortlessly.

I am not a psychologist or a psychiatrist, and experts were not consulted; however, sometimes experience is worth the price of therapy. And trust me, I feel like I've had a few hundred g's worth of experience!

All of the scenarios presented are *based* upon real-life experiences—both mine and those of other people in my life. I've changed all of the names and altered some of the situational details, in the hope of using my own experiences as representative examples to help my readers with their journeys through this Wack-y world. Hopefully, these scenarios and the analyses that follow will give you, my reader, the tools you need to protect yourself from the warped and the wicked.

Furthermore, I am well aware that many Wacko characteristics can be the result of mental or physical illnesses, former or current abusive relationships or traumatic events left unchecked or untreated. And, quite honestly, some people are just born on the wrong side of the bed. This book doesn't go into great detail to explore the reasons behind the Wacko behavior; I'll leave that for the professionals. And, frankly, I've had my fill of books that effectively excuse Wackoness by delving into childhoods of early potty training and classroom rivalries. My reason for writing this book is to focus on the needs of the wronged, rather than the excuses of the wicked. So I've created this book about spotting Wacko characteristics to help the peacekeepers among us recognize these people and counter—or, better yet, avoid—their attacks. Life can be a solemn and heavy trip. My goal was to write a sometimes humorous book about some not-so-funny behavior that many of us have tolerated for far too long. Consider this book your first financial investment in the journey to a Wacko-free world. As they say in the military: know thine enemy.

Between the covers of this book lies an extravaganza of scenarios involving Wackos of varying degrees. If any of these stories or character profiles start sounding familiar, then this book is for you. Allow me to throw you my own personal life raft of advice. Enjoy!

Part One

"True happiness consists not in the multitude of friends, but in their worth and choice."

—*Samuel Johnson (1709–1784), British lexicographer*

1 The Nasty Habits of Hosting Wackos

I have two goals for this book: (1) to help you identify and deal with the Wackos in your life; and (2) to help you recognize those traits within yourself that could actually be drawing Wackos to you. We can't prevent Wackos from crossing our paths in life, but we can discourage them from attaching themselves to us when they do.

Ask yourself these questions:

▶ Do strangers spill their life stories (often in embarrassingly graphic detail) within minutes of meeting me?

▶ Have I spent my life helping people, being a good friend and more than periodically pulling the knife out of my back? Does my life lack balance?

▶ Do I spend hours listening to "friends" and their problems only to be cut off when I try to share my own?

▶ Does my life lack balance?

▶ How many times have I wondered, *What is it with me? Do I have an invisible sign on my back that says, 'The confessional is open'?*

Think about your answers to these questions and the emotions that stirred within you when you pondered them.

Now for my final question:

▶ Do you think you might be hosting way too many Wackos?

If so, read on.

What my very informal Wacko research revealed is that people who tend to take advantage of every real and perceived act of hospitality seem to home in on those who don't mind playing the part of host. Likewise, people who are pushovers tend to have a lot of very "pushy" friends. It's the unavoidable magnet-and-steel attraction. In fact, to refer to Wacko hosting as a "habit" as I do in the title of this chapter is misleading. It goes beyond habit. It's biology. But it is possible to tweak your natural tendencies and become a tad choosier when it comes to forming friendships. Think of yourself as a magnet capable of turning off your magnetism when the situation requires it. Once you learn how to do this, you'll break the cycle of attracting Wackos. However, you may endure numerous Wacko encounters before you completely master this skill. I know I did.

My therapist once told me, "Christina, until you stand up to people who have the characteristics that represent the person in your life you are running away from, expect the universe to present them to you time and time again." She was right, but it's much easier said than done. Standing up to people is *not* one of my strong suits. I am non-confrontational by nature, as are most of us who attract Wackos. We "hosts" are so busy being kind and forgiving of all irritating behavior that we allow others to take advantage of us, and we do nothing about it. Beneath the surface, we might hear whispers of discontent and bewilderment, but on the surface, we make excuses for the Wacko and forgive and forget. Let's face it; it's much easier to be nice to everyone than to engage in conflict. Wackos seem to recognize this trait, which they perceive as weakness. Host traits are not weaknesses at all when the host surrounds herself with true friends—not those who seek to exploit her kindness. For simplicity reasons, I tend to refer to "hosts" as female, but bear in mind that everything I discuss can be applied to both genders.

If you have a host in your life, take this friend out to lunch once a month, call, build a shrine in his or her honor and always nurture that relationship. They don't grow on trees, as dear old Mom used to say. After I extracted myself from my horrendous business partnership with Maureen, my dear friend Savannah told me in her sweet Southern accent, "Christina, there ah two kinds of people in this world: Shahks and dolphins. Shahks will never change. They love to take a bite out of sweet meat. Their black, fathomless eyes roll back in their head as they do it! They feel nothing as they tear you apaht and kill paht of your spirit. Then, when they think they have destroyed you, they will swim away looking for their next person to take a bite out of. You ah a dolphin; stop swimming with the shahks! Now, if you aren't going to call that Wacko and tell her what a bitch she is, give me that number and I'll call the bitch myself!" Everyone needs a Savannah in her life, and I cherish mine.

We hosts have made second careers out of saving people because it's part of our nature, but we need saviors, too. When I met my husband, I knew he was the savior for me. He was strong-willed, respectful of women, smart as a whip and a huge daddy figure, which was just what I needed eighteen years ago and still do today. He is always there to protect me and tell me when a Wacko is knocking on my door. Of course, until I was hit by the two-by-four I didn't listen closely enough, but he was always there to help me clean up the debris after the storm. My point is: cherish those people in your life who are your true supporters, and learn to purge your life of those who aren't.

2 What Wackos Look For

Most hosts possess all or some of the following traits. Could any of these expressions apply to you?

> *Mother Teresa is My Middle Name*
> *I'm Afraid to Stand in My Personal Power*
> *Laughter is My Defense Mechanism*
> *I'm Apologetic to a Fault*
> *I Can't Handle Compliments*

If so, keep reading.

Mother Teresa Takes It All On

Those possessing what I call the Mother Teresa Syndrome want the world to love and accept them, and they can and will exhaust themselves achieving this. I've labeled this particular characteristic a "syndrome" because it's actually the embodiment of many sub-traits. Mother Teresas are consummate best friends, pleasers, saviors and tight-lipped confidants. Most Wacko-attracting hosts are up to their spine-deficient necks in this trait.

Kari is a prime example. She embodies nearly every facet of the Mother Teresa Syndrome. A stay-at-home mother of three, Kari will go to great lengths to help someone—not only for love and acceptance, but also because it is a natural, instinctive response for her. God sent her here for that reason. Pleasing others, being the best friend she can be, listening to personal details for hours on end, being loyal and keeping secrets are part of her character. She does all of this while being the ever-attentive wife and mother. She is shiny and polished like a new shoe. She doesn't have to work hard at any of this. She just oozes it.

Kari listens to her friends' problems while she's on the toilet because she can't say, "I need to use the bathroom; do you mind if I call you back?" She can't hang up because she is *so* needed. What she fails to realize or just can't admit to herself is that the person talking to her ad infinitum is slowly sucking the energy from her soul and will continue to do so until 4 in the morning—or until Kari passes out, whichever comes first. Because of Kari's acute Mother Teresa Syndrome, she can't muster the gumption to hang up.

What better way to talk behind the backs of everyone than to vent to a living, breathing information lockbox?

Why does Kari's Wacko friend talk her ear off? How did this situation become so lopsided? Because Kari inadvertently gives her friend the green light. Kari will listen for hours without interrupting, and she will never repeat a thing she is told. Ever. Kari's Mother Teresa Syndrome acts as a natural buffer against the blabbermouth bug. Kari will never spill. I call this the Confidentiality Agreement. This is a fabulous attribute to possess within a circle of true friends, but when a Wacko gets wind of it, he or she will see it as a personal safety net. What better way to talk behind the backs of everyone in your life than to vent to a living, breathing information lockbox? I'm not saying that Kari should start sharing intimate details with the general public. I'm hoping that in the future, she won't let the situation progress this far from the start.

There is an old saying, *How it begins is how it ends*. Remember and repeat this principle when you hear yourself making excuses. Recognizing a hopeless situation, from the start, is the key to escaping unharmed.

My next two examples illustrate two concepts. One's that our Mother Teresa Syndrome can prove disruptive even if no Wacko is involved. The other's that we begin developing the traits within this syndrome early in life.

When I was in high school, I dated a guy from one of the military academies. I was eighteen, and he was twenty–two. This guy had everything going for him: first in his graduating class and tall, blonde and handsome. Charming, too. To top it all off, he was crazy about me. For some reason, though, I just wasn't physically attracted to him, so I told him I was Catholic and didn't believe in premarital sex. He believed me, and that was good enough to end things. Why did I allow this relationship to continue past its expiration date? Because being "Mother Teresa, the Pleaser," I couldn't let down the woman who introduced us. I had to like this guy because he was *her* pride and joy. Thank God we didn't get married, or I would have had to come up with some other religion that believes in decade after decade of abstinence. That whole process lasted more than a year, and it wasn't fair to waste that poor guy's time or my own.

Let's take things to a whole different level. I had a dream that I was in college and a handsome football player asked me out. The anticipation was building as I waited for my date to ring my doorbell; even in my dream state I could feel my belly flutter. I was exuding sexuality and confidence. I was dressed to kill in a black silk Gucci number. Then, I opened the door. Standing before me was a Greek god of a man wearing a dress, high heels, wig and makeup and carrying a purse. Now, most well-adjusted individuals would break into laughter or accuse their date of playing the funniest joke they had ever seen. Not me. Even in my dream, my fragile self-esteem was evident. I was thinking, *Oh my God, his makeup looks better than mine!* I then proceeded to say, "I'm sorry for staring. You look very nice." One can be a pleaser even in a dream state.

To ask if a Mother Teresa type has a tough time saying "no" is like asking if the sky is blue or, as my college pal and I would say, "Does George scratch?" He was a professor we had who would stand in front of the class and pick his privates.

Those with the Mother Teresa Syndrome have a compulsion to please everyone except themselves. Learning to embrace and wield the word "no" would be a monumental leap in the right direction. It's OK to say, "No, thank you." My five-year-old says it all the time!

And it is certainly all right to want to please others, but it's not necessary to waste a year of your life dating the wrong person like yours truly did. And it's not all right to take the phone into the throne a la Kari rather than interrupt a friend's monolog.

If you feel as if you are repeatedly sacrificing yourself for someone else, then the sitch ain't right.

Afraid To Stand in Personal Power

I suspect that most hosts were raised in one family extreme or the other. Kari, for instance, was raised by Brady Bunch clones, surrounded by 24/7 love and support and perfect teeth. Ergo, she couldn't sense an abuser coming based on experience. When you're wrapped in familial arms full of devotion and protection for most of your life, it's hard to imagine being treated any other way.

At the opposite end of the family spectrum exists a non-supportive environment, where accomplishments idle unacknowledged and put-downs pepper every verbal transaction. It's been my personal experience that hosts raised in a home life similar to this have developed traits of extreme generosity to overcompensate for what their lives at home lacked.

Either way, Kari and other hosts have tremendous difficulty standing in their personal power; therefore, they are easily exploited by Wacko types. It's as if they're exuding a pheromone that makes people want to use them for target practice.

Symptomatic of this particular trait is a need to wait endlessly for people. Sound familiar? Kari will wait for her companion to show up until the restaurant closes. If her friend is an hour late, she might be a little angry, but for the most part her mind will go places other minds don't. She might rehash the last phone conversation or email message that she exchanged with her friend and think that she said something offensive. Kari might also think that suddenly the person doesn't like her or that she forgot about their commitment. Never would it occur to Kari that the person she planned to meet is simply too rude to be on time—or decided to blow off the commitment altogether. The dead giveaway that Kari is mired in this trait is when Kari's beyond-fashionably-late companion offers a cavalier apology, and Kari instantly forgives her. A part of Kari is furious because she knows her dear "friend" is parading around town with a cell phone glued to her ear most of the time, but apparently, she can't dial Kari's number to say she's running late. But, Kari will struggle 'til the end of time to suppress this anger. *After all,* she thinks to herself, *why ruin what could be a lovely meal?* Well, I'll tell her why. Because this situation will repeat itself until the end of time if she allows it. Kari's inability to stand in her own power has put her in the same bind as her Mother Teresa Syndrome: by always waiting endlessly, she is giving the Wackos in her life the green light to take advantage of her.

Kari will wait for phone calls as well. I know how debilitating this can be because I used to do it, too. It wasn't until I paid $500 for a seminar that I learned that my time is just as valuable as everyone else's. Save your money and just take my advice: wait no longer than thirty minutes for anyone. If they care, they'll find a way to call. If they don't show up or call, get on with your day—and your life. If they're truly friends, they'll forgive you for leaving. People either respect you or they don't. If they don't, they're history. That's it.

Laughter Is Her Captor

Who wouldn't want to hang around with Kari? She is so happy-go-lucky she could give Mary Poppins lessons in optimism. Almost nothing offends her, she sees the sunny side of any dark cloud, and her laughter is infectious. Because laughter is another way for Kari to make people happy, she feels she must always laugh, no matter what the circumstances. In the midst of a lousy personal situation, laughing at herself is critical to her emotional fortitude. It's her survival mechanism. A Wacko friend can make unflattering comments about Kari's clothing or belittle her home's décor, and she will laugh right along with the crowd. She would never risk spoiling someone else's fun. What Kari may subconsciously suspect but still struggles to admit in therapy is that her laughter is not erasing the negative emotions stirring within; it is only concealing them—and temporarily at that. If you've ever known someone like this, you know how easily she is used for target practice.

I, for one, identify particularly closely with this host trait. Hosts cannot reveal to others that they are troubled. We simply cannot bear the thought of being a "burden" to anyone. The stress of being in the business relationship with Maureen took its toll on me, and I suffered a miscarriage. But I couldn't reveal my suffering to others. I didn't want to risk "bringing everyone else down." I made such light of this personal tragedy that my twelve-year-old daughter, Paris, confronted me and accused me of not going through the grieving process. It's pitiful when your own children are more mature that you are. Anyway, this little person who comes up to my breastbone said, "Mom, you are not dealing with this. You keep making light of this, and you have not grieved. Mom, this is serious and you need to grieve because it really has affected you. You aren't the same." After this, I cried on her shoulder so long and so hard that we had to wring out her shirt.

Hosts need to laugh all the time or they feel out of body. I'm convinced that most actors and comedians exemplify this particular trait.

Real friends will accept (and expect) real emotions. Don't rub shoulders with people who won't let you cry on theirs.

Apologetic to a Fault

Some hosts are classic "I'm sorry" people. Those with this trait will apologize for everything down to the sun not rising fast enough. "I'm sorry that the dog got hair on your pants." "I'm sorry the weather is bad." "I'm sorry you stepped on *my* foot and broke *my toe!*" People like this feel out of balance if they can't squeeze an apology into every conversation. We all know people like this, and we all know that it's annoying. So if you're guilty of owning this trait, pay close attention.

I recently called my attorney and apologized for calling her with a question. When I shared this particular moment of insanity with Savannah, her response was, "Noooo, noooo. Tell me you didn't, puh-leeze! That is really pathetic, Christina." My first response was, "I know. I'm so sorry I did that to myself." Miss Apologetic is a close cousin of Mother Teresa, the Pleaser. She probably learned to be overly apologetic early in life as a way of avoiding conflict, and if this habit is not nipped in the bud it will continue well into adulthood.

I once went to Mexico with my Russian-born friend Ilsa and her family for Thanksgiving. I said "I'm sorry" so many times that finally Ilsa looked at me and asked in her Russian accent, "Oh my God, what are you going to do, hang yourself in the bathroom?" This was over running out of toilet paper. Ilsa says what's on her mind, and for that I am thankful.

Hosts must learn to wield their apologies carefully. This trait is an easy one for Wackos to exploit. After all, if you're the apologetic sponge absorbing the blame for everything, what does your Wacko friend have to worry about? If you tend to fall into the category of being apologetic to a fault, think for a minute about the responses you've gotten from the receiver(s) of your apologies. These responses are the keys to distinguishing true friends from cleverly disguised Wackos.

When you say "I'm sorry" to someone and she says, "Don't worry about it; an apology isn't necessary," she's worthy of your presence. When you say you are sorry to someone and she responds by sitting in silence and not acknowledging your apology, whip out your psychological forceps and extract yourself from that relationship. I once ditched a Level 3 Wacko who would sit in silence any time I apologized to her, which would make me feel bad for days. Wackos seem to think that there's an invisible scoreboard somewhere, and that their adolescent-level power trips are earning them points. Don't let them win.

When I finally began standing in my personal power, I decided that people are not worthy of my apologies if their hearts aren't open to receive them.

Try to hold back on your apologies until one is really warranted. My suggestion is to not go over three a day unless it is absolutely necessary. If you owe someone an apology and you are about to go over your limit, explain the situation and tell the other person she will be first on your list tomorrow. If she loves you, she will wait.

Please Don't Pass the Compliments

It's my theory that because some hosts didn't receive an abundance of compliments during childhood, they find it difficult to accept them as adults. Children can never get enough compliments, and those of you out there who aren't stroking your kids' egos will pay the shrink bills later. And sometimes a host simply develops her own aversion to compliments because she's convinced that she's the one who's supposed to be praising everyone else. This is Kari's problem.

When someone starts complimenting Kari, she breaks into a cold, nervous sweat. She is the one who is supposed to be doing the complimenting—to keep those around her happy, of course. By God, don't turn the tables on her! The compliments don't boost Kari's self-esteem; in her mind, they only paint an impossible ideal she cannot meet.

When Kari finally becomes so emotionally wilted that she does accept a compliment, it means she really needed it.

Occasionally, after she's waved off a decade's worth of compliments, it will catch up to her and she'll suddenly need nonstop reassurance. She will need to be told one hundred times that she made the right decision, that her hair looks great, that her new curtains look great, etc. It's as if she didn't hear the praise the first ninety–nine times.

I think most of us have witnessed (or been guilty of) this type of behavior before. It's hard to not get frustrated when someone doesn't accept your compliment gracefully. Don't get angry with the Kari in your life; pay her the same praise one hundred times if you have to, because she has absolutely given more than she has ever gotten.

After being in therapy and understanding how uncomfortable I felt accepting praise, I have learned to *try* to accept it. I smile and say a quick "Thank you." My advice would be to start doing the same right now. Break the nasty cycle by simply saying "Thank you." Period. Don't editorialize with any "Yeah right. You're just saying that to make me feel better" stuff. It annoys people, and their compliments go unacknowledged. And, like an apology, if your heart can't be open to receive a compliment, sooner or later people will stop giving them to you.

If your tipsy friend is relentless, you might have to excuse yourself for a "timeout."

Recently, my pal Angela opened her home for a women's weekend. Ilsa, Savannah and I arrived and broke out the champagne as Angela's gourmet chef husband, David, made sushi for the gang. Savannah had two glasses of champagne and started idolizing me, or, at least that was how I felt. She wouldn't stop going on and on about what a good friend I was to her, how I have always been there for her, etc. At first I smiled and said "Thank you," but she wouldn't stop. Those of you with an aversion to accepting compliments can relate to my squirminess and discomfort. If you've done your best to accept a compliment, but your tipsy friend is relentless, you might have to excuse yourself for a "timeout." Another tactic is to try changing the subject. I took advantage of that tip and started to repeat a story I had told about five times already. That did it. I knew if Savannah heard the story again she would vomit profusely. So, every time she praised me I would interrupt and start the story, and she would stop.

When I had first arrived at Angela's, my friends were apologizing for the most pathetic things, so right away I laid down a quota. This apology quota, combined with my strategy to curb Savannah's compliments got her attention. "Wait a minute," said Savannah with her dramatic, exasperated Southern accent, "I'm not allowed to compliment you, and I can't say I'm sorry. What am I allowed to do?"

True friends, like my Savannah, will learn to respect your boundaries.

All of these host traits are easy for predatory Wackos to exploit. You may have discovered that some or perhaps all apply to you or someone you know. Someone who desires to only please others, who refuses to harness her personal power, laughs off any derogatory remarks or situations, apologizes profusely and does not feel worthy of compliments amounts to one major Wacko magnet. It's time to remove that target that's taped to your back and learn some defensive maneuvers.

3 Getting Hit by the Two-by-Four

Say it with me: *How it begins is how it ends.*

If we could plop down in front of our televisions and view a retrospective documentary of our failed friendships, we would probably be able to spot the clues that existed all along. Like those mildly hurtful comments—you know the ones—the ones you shrugged off saying, "I'm sure she didn't mean it to sound that way." And you would also notice the disrespectful actions—the tardiness, the phone calls right at dinnertime and the broken promises. It's easy to overlook these transgressions in the midst of what we construe to be a friendship. And therein lies the root of problem: we're exhausting ourselves trying to befriend virtually everyone we meet, and we've lost our sense of what constitutes a true friendship. At some point in our lives, we started ranking quantity above quality.

But don't worry. Even the most charitable of Wacko hosts won't put up and shut up forever. The two-by-four will strike, and when it does, I want you to be prepared to accept the wake-up call and purge your parasites.

Remember Kari, our quintessential host? She was finally struck by the two-by-four when she went shopping with a Wacko. While they were browsing at housewares, Kari spotted a striking bowl they both wanted. There were two of them left and both women simultaneously noticed a flaw in the porcelain of one of them. Even though Kari discovered the treasure, she stood there silently as her "friend" grabbed the good one and left her with the bad. She even stared Kari down with a look that said "If you aren't going to say something, I'm taking it." Kari felt deeply disturbed on her drive home, and rightfully so. The Wacko knew what she was doing and did it anyway, knowing Kari wouldn't protest. In a flash of clarity as she drove herself and her flawed bowl home, Kari suddenly understood her disturbing co-dependence and knew it was time to say good-bye to her so-called friend.

I could speculate about what Kari should have done differently when baited by her friend, but that would be a waste of gray matter. A true friend wouldn't have put Kari in that situation. Instead, I will venture that this incident probably wasn't the first of its kind. I would wager that this particular Wacko made a habit of testing Kari's personal power. Had Kari carefully watched, looked and listened from the beginning of her relationship with this person (more on this important technique in Chapter 4), I've no doubt she would have spotted the crimson flags. To this day, when Kari uses that flawed bowl she is reminded of the day of her awakening and that it is OK to speak your mind.

The day I was struck by the two-by-four was a bit more dramatic—perhaps because my situation was a tad more complex than buying a bowl.

I'm not shopping for anyone's sympathy—I entered into my business partnership with my eyes and checkbook wide open—I just want others to learn from my example.

When I accepted Maureen's business proposition, I broke my cardinal rule: I truly believed I would be different. I would be the one true friend of hers with whom she would share a relationship of mutual trust and respect. I wouldn't receive the same treatment I'd watched her dish out to others because I was a good friend and listened to her blabber for hours on end for two years. She wouldn't dare bite the hand that fed her ego a steady diet of sympathy, compliments and patience, would she?

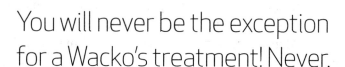

You will never be the exception for a Wacko's treatment! Never.

This brings us to another mantra worth repeating over and over: *You will never be the exception for a Wacko's treatment. Never.*

My sensibilities seemed to be intact on so many other levels. Yet, I ignored that tiny voice inside me that was cautioning me against such an arrangement with Maureen. Being casual friends is one thing: a binding, business investment is something else entirely.

What hooked me on this business venture was the fact that Maureen actually had a good idea—a really good idea. We were going to launch a line of pet products—shampoos designed for different dog breeds, to be exact. The idea had merit and the whole concept of starting and growing a business from scratch sounded therapeutic—like a brand new beginning. Still, the uneasy voice inside me grew louder.

I can still remember standing in my driveway, my eyes fixed in astonishment and my jaw hanging as Maureen drove away with a smile, saying, "Get the whole thing put together, Christina! I'll be back from Mexico in ten days!" Mexico? Feeling suddenly like an island, I managed to move forward and got the business ready to launch according to our conversations. What was I thinking? My guess is, I wasn't. I was *feeling* charitable; I was *feeling* a need to believe in this project. But *thinking*? No way.

Eventually, I had to face what my subconscious had known would happen all along: an eruption of catastrophic proportions. In conversations with friends, I likened my awakening to the spontaneous eruption of a previously inactive volcano. All the doubts, all the suspicions I'd buried beneath the surface suddenly shot skyward and came crashing down upon me.

When I was hit by the two-by-four, I was hit and hit *hard*.

Maureen and I had just finished exhibiting our products at a week-long trade show in Reno. Our business was poised to boom, but a week with Maureen had started to wear my patience thin. If she weren't in the women's room preening, she was extolling the virtues of *her* business. Not *ours*. Hers. She wasn't appreciative of the time and work I'd spent getting our products and business prepared. In fact, she acted as though she'd rather I wasn't there at all.

After the trade show ended, we stopped by a local restaurant before heading to the airport to fly home. I was trying my best to stay focused on our business and on the orders that we needed to fill from the trade show. There we sat, as different as chateaubriand and an Oscar Mayer wiener. I understood that I needed to look the part of a successful businessperson, so I was dressed in an attractive suit and was very careful with my hair and makeup. Maureen, however, was her typical underdressed, over-inflated self. Her acute adult acne detracted from most of her features, with the exception of her exaggerated under-bite, which made her resemble a bulldog. (Now, I know acne is a horrible problem for some. Just indulge my sharp tongue when it comes to Maureen. She constantly held every aspect of my existence under a microscope; I need some vindication.)

I'm sure we were quite a sight.

I didn't have to say much during dinner. Maureen kept talking and talking about *her* vision, *her* ideas, *her* business, and suddenly, I had the sensation that her voice was coming from somewhere far away. I watched her mouth move; I watched her teeth chew and grind and pulverize her food. Her voice became more distant and unintelligible. I think I stopped blinking. I know I stopped eating. She was so wrapped up in herself; I'm surprised she remembered I was still there.

I knew the conversation was heading south when she professed to have an abundance of business acumen and that my lack thereof was holding her back professionally.

"Christina, I don't want to hurt your feelings," she slurred between wads of prime rib, "but I'm a businesswoman and you are just a housewife." I confess that I'm no Einstein, but I do have two college degrees and have climbed quite high up on a few corporate ladders in my day. Maureen, on the other hand, is a high school dropout with no advanced education. It wasn't the label "housewife" that I found offensive; I'm very proud of the choice that I made. But what I did find insulting was her slimy delivery—the way she made "housewife" sound like it was one generation removed from being a troglodyte. Her insolence suddenly reeled me back to reality. "What do you want Christina? I'll buy you out," she said flatly.

When I heard her babble the words "I'll buy you out," the two-by-four smacked me right between the eyes: she had never wanted a partner. She wanted someone to do the legwork, smooth out the kinks and then hand her a ball she could run with—or complain about.

That's when the top of the volcano blew off. I could almost see the mushroom cloud forming right above our table. Then I could feel it—the burning and stinging of the lava as it rained down upon me. Why in the world had I let her talk me into this? I wanted to speak, but I was afraid of choking on the ash and smoke. There were so many thoughts and emotions swirling around in my head, and it took me a moment to compose myself.

When I was ready, I calmly told her that a buyout would be fine. She put her fork down, apparently realizing that I was finally listening, and absentmindedly fingered a massive zit on her chin. She stared evenly at me for a moment and then dove back into her meal as if nothing had happened.

Physically ill from tolerating her for six days, I was relieved to be handed such an amicable way out. But I didn't get rid of her quite so easily, as you will discover later on in this book.

I'm not sure what's more disturbing: the ease with which she hoodwinked someone who tried to be her friend, or the ease with which her wannabe friend took the bait.

How it began was how it ended—with Maureen riding into the sunset and me left standing in disbelief.

Harnessing the Power

I started standing in my power in my mid-thirties, and that seems to be the case among all of my close friends—male and female alike. Hosts don't sense the depth of their internal power (probably because it was seldom tapped) until they get hit on the head with a two-by-four and feel the blood running down their faces. At the point when a host is mopping the blood from her face, watch out. It's unfortunate that hosts have to endure repeated Wacko experiences before they finally get pissed enough to unleash their pent-up power. The last Wacko in my life did it for me; no more crazies for me. When we have been pushed too far, we come out fighting. Once we conjure up our power and call the scoundrels on their stuff, they scurry. Personal power is in there, and it's usually one of the higher levels of Wackos that will bring it out in us.

> Personal power is in there, and it's usually one of the higher levels of Wackos that will bring it out in us.

Hosts don't have to wait for the two-by-four to strike if they don't want to. The challenge is harnessing the power to give a Wacko the boot without the benefit of adrenaline from a calamitous situation.

I've always maintained that Wackos are actually threatened by hosts. After all, it's the host who's holding all the cards—even if he or she is not aware of it. So, I'm making you aware of it now! A parasite cannot survive without a host. Once you determine what it is the Wacko in your life is gaining from your relationship, try withholding it, and the parasite will be forced to move on. If you're always getting stuck with the lunch tab, for instance, find another dining partner. You might have to work hard at first to avoid situations in which you're easily exploited. It's a small step, but it's one that's headed in the right direction. Even if the Wacko remains in your life, you will have the pleasure of knowing that you are no longer feeding his or her Wacko appetite. And, most importantly, you are using your personal power to take control of the situation before it evolves into a recurring nightmare.

Kari would have made huge strides toward ridding herself of the Wackos in her life had she harnessed the power to simply speak her truth. Telling a friend that she needs to end a phone conversation and staking her claim on the perfect bowl would have been well within her rights. By learning to speak her truth in a firm way, without anger or judgment, she could have spared herself a lot of grief by either eliminating the Wackos from her life or by earning their respect in the end.

Have you ever awakened on a sunny morning and felt totally in your power? That's your suppressed, internal strength striving to break through. So go with it. Call all of your buddies and say, "Wow, I'm at the top of my game today. I've had a breakthrough! I'm going to do this; I'm going to do that." And when you wake up the next day and your subconscious mind, which runs on habit, says, "Man, what were you thinking? You can't do something for yourself; you need to do things for other people," don't listen to it. Flex your personal power muscles and push those habitual doubts aside. I realize that this sounds easier than it is. I understand. For most hosts, myself included, standing in our personal power was not instilled during childhood and to actually do so is monumental. Reward yourself for the tiniest accomplishments.

Chapter 4
Watch, Look and Listen

In all my years of being in personal and professional relationships, I have found that hosts are the best friends you could ever have. They are loyal, honest confidants who will move mountains to help you in any problem situation. The only downside of *being* a host is that your traits can be exploited. I believe I attracted so many Wackos because, since childhood, I was in the habit of trying to please people—all people—for love and acceptance. It wasn't until my mid-thirties when I learned to really watch, look and listen to the people around me that I felt truly safe and empowered for the first time in my life. It was like coming out of the fog.

"Watch, look and listen" is a directive you will hear repeatedly in this book. **Watch** the big picture unfolding before you, and really **look** closely at the people in your life—at their actions and the choices they make. **Listening** is twofold. Listen to and process what you hear them say about themselves and others, and above all, listen to your own inner voice.

I remember with great pride the first time I put my new philosophy into practice. We had just moved into a new home, and one of the neighbors threw a cocktail party. I met a man (we'll call him Sean) who shared mine and Ched's passion for hiking. We all met the next morning, and we hiked for two hours. I barely uttered a word. I listened. And I learned. Sean politely put down some of his closest "friends" and colleagues.

"Gary is great, but he doesn't know the industry the way I do;" "Taylor doesn't have a whole lot going on upstairs, but I like him anyway." I knew right then and there that he would put down me (and/or Ched) in the same fashion—it was our choice whether or not to provide him with any ammunition. We chose to socialize casually with Sean without revealing anything personal. We weren't about to give him any dirt for his shovel, although I figured he would find fault with the way I breathed or the way Ched's eyelids blinked if that's what he had to resort to. Ched and I maintained a two-year relationship with him anyway, because if we wanted a good hike we knew whom to call. You see, you can choose how to relate to Wackos—how far you are willing to let them into your world. Just don't start boo-hooing if you get burned in the process—you know what they say about playing with fire. This man would never be a true friend to either one of us, and we knew we would not be the exception to the rule. We never told Sean anything we didn't want the world to know. The simple process of watch, look and listen had given us the upper hand—we were holding all the cards. Finally, after a significant passage of time Sean blatantly came out and practically demanded information. We still kept our mouths shut. In the end, when we moved away, Sean asked if we were in the witness protection program.

Part Two

"Forgive your enemies, but never forget their names."

—*John F. Kennedy*

5 Dissecting
Wacko Behavior

Wackos come in all packages and strengths. They may have emerged from backgrounds of affluence or poverty—as an only child or as part of a large brood. In any case, Wackos seem to feel better only after they've succeeded in making someone else feel worse. There is much Wacko behavior to be wary of—some of it highly destructive and some of it just plain inconsiderate.

I've created a hierarchy of ascending Wacko levels—the lowest of which may be tolerable in certain situations and for short intervals, and the highest of which would prove to be unbearable after a minimal amount of interaction.

> Both hosts and Wackos can emerge from similar home environments.

Interestingly enough, both hosts and Wackos can emerge from similar home environments. A friend I grew up with had strong, overbearing parents. My friend was a classic host, and her sister was a classic Wacko. In this case, I would imagine that the Wacko sister was trying to overcompensate for the sense of powerlessness that she felt at home by acting like she had the world by the horns. Conversely, the host sister (my friend) had a tough time unleashing her true spirit.

Of course, Wackos can emerge from any family background; I use the overbearing parents as just one example.

When I said that hosts are the ones holding all the cards, I was telling the truth. Wackos aren't all-powerful beings; they just want people to *think* that they are. Wackos bury their demons by convincing the world that they've got it together. But, when hosts learn to stand in their personal power and stop a Wacko in his or her tracks, there's not a darn thing the Wacko can do about it, other than head off in search of another victim.

Wackos Have Health Problems

I have observed that Wackos have a propensity toward health problems—sooner or later. Scientific research has shown a biological connection between a positive outlook and resistance to diseases. In a nutshell, happy people are healthy people. I believe it, and you should too. *Real* happy people. Not *pretend* happy people. A lot of Wackos pretend to be happy with their lives. Perhaps on some level they believe it's true. There are plenty of perfectly manicured lawns and upscale Tudor facades that serve only to hide internal household dysfunction. But all that camouflaging doesn't do a bit of good when it comes to physiology. We've all heard that suppressed emotions—anger, resentment, fear and confusion about our feelings in general—can manifest themselves as health problems. Wackos are not immune to this reality.

I can vividly recall being at a friend's house as a child and watching her older Wacko brother arguing with his controlling parent. He struggled mightily to stand his ground and not let the parent control him. Finally, the kid lost the battle and fainted. At the time, I really didn't know what to make of what I had witnessed. My friend called later and informed me that her thirteen-year-old brother had seen a doctor and was diagnosed with anemia. The notion that health problems related to Wacko tendencies can appear so early on is disturbing, to say the least. Just think of what this guy must be dealing with as an adult.

My dear friend, Suzanne has an older sister whom you will read more about later. Sarah mistreated Suzanne throughout their childhood and partway into adulthood. I would classify Sarah as a Wacko 1. The last time Suzanne saw Sarah, Sarah had put on about fifty pounds and had a severe skin condition covering most of her body. When negativity is held in captivity for too long, it eventually must break free—and not in a good way.

And remember my nemesis, Maureen? Her skin is so mottled and pocked by acne (which she confided in me is worse when she's under stress), I'm surprised an orbiting shuttle hasn't attempted a lunar landing smack on her proboscis.

The Insuperable Apron Strings

I knew a Wacko who could not overcome the entrapments of his overbearing, control-freak parents. He actually ended up *marrying* an overbearing control freak. It's not that far-fetched when you think about it. Controlling behavior is all the Wacko has known his entire life, and on some subconscious level, it's what he's comfortable with. It provides consistency.

Wackos will take this stroll down the matrimonial aisle without realizing what they have done to themselves.

I also knew a Wacko 1 from work named Katrina. It was not unusual for Katrina to "tattle" on other employees. She would walk into our boss's office and preface her gossip with something like, "You might want to know this, boss," or "Gosh, I feel so uncomfortable telling you this, but...." She also seemed to enjoy finding all of her friends' weaknesses and discussing them with other friends. Before I realized that she was a Wacko, Katrina and I had a brief friendship during which I learned a lot about her. She had left home at eighteen and paid her way through college, working every job she could juggle. She graduated and landed a great job in the city (where I met her). She seemed to really be soaring in her personal life and in her career. Eventually, however, she was drawn to a man who treated her just as her father had: with little attention and even less affection. Katrina's mother died when Katrina was just a child, and Katrina said that her father became emotionally withdrawn. She once told me that the first and only time that her father said the words "I love you" was when Katrina was lying in a hospital bed after an attempted suicide.

Katrina married the man she met in the city, most likely because he treated her the way she was used to being treated. It didn't take family members long to see that the husband, although he seemed nice, was also unaffectionate and didn't care much for conversation. If Katrina weren't such a bitch, I'd feel sorry for her. But she is a Wacko 1, remember? You can feel sorry for Wackos who fall into these parent-produced traps, but don't engage by putting out a helping hand. A Wacko most likely would never admit that help was needed anyway. The funny thing is, Wackos will stay in these relationships until the bitter end, wallowing in their own misery, but trying like heck to paint a perfect picture for the rest of the world to see. They're just repeating their own parents' behavior by hiding behind a pleasant pretense.

Sometimes a Wacko can actually become so dependent upon a parent's controlling behavior that he doesn't know how to act or live without it.

Sometimes a Wacko can actually become so dependent upon a parent's controlling behavior that he doesn't know how to act or live without it.

A Wacko 1 whom I once knew named John was raised by a domineering mother. John's mother tried to run nearly every aspect of his life, making decisions for him both big and small. After John married, his mother incorrectly assumed that she would be gaining a daughter-in-law she could control as well. When her struggles to manipulate John's wife fell flat, she turned to John for backup. When John took his wife's side and stood up to his mother, she would cease her relations with him until he would come crawling back with an apology. I had witnessed John's yo-yo routine several times before I decided to voice my opinion. I was in therapy at the time and could see with great clarity what was happening. "Don't you think that it's terribly unreasonable that your mother is trying so hard to control your wife? Isn't this causing a lot of angst between you and your wife?" I asked.

He looked at me as if I were a stranger. He said, "You don't understand. If I stand up to my mother, she'll cut me off. I can't deal with that!"

Poor John. His mother's apron strings had him in a chokehold. Most Wackos cannot harness the power to break free; in fact, I'm not even sure that they want to break free. The co-dependence nurtured for so many years by the controlling parent(s) is an unhealthy bond—but a sticky bond just the same.

I've presented these two major downsides of "Wackohood" not to drum up sympathy for Wackos, but rather, so that you will have a greater understanding of what goes on behind the scenes in a Wacko's life. Armed with this information, you may find it within your heart to forgive the Wackos who have crossed your path in life and caused you harm. Forgiving is the first step toward moving on.

Now, onto our ladder of Wacko levels.

6 Characteristics of a Wacko 1

The most tolerable of all Wacko levels is Wacko 1 (W1). Those who have developed into W1s were probably teetering on the psychological fence at some point in their lives, and they could have fallen either way—they could have developed into demur, world-pleasing hosts, or they could have evolved into budding Wackos. We learned earlier that Wackos and hosts both have trouble standing in their personal power. The big difference between how hosts and Wackos handle this trait, however, is that Wackos will move heaven and earth to overcompensate for their power deficiency. In its place, they will develop other behaviors that give the illusion of power.

A W1 often exhibits the following characteristics:

I Do No Wrong
I'm a Tattletale
I Brandish a Sharp Tongue
I Have Difficulty Giving Affection
I'm Antisocial

I Do No Wrong

One core trait is universal among all Wacko levels and is the well from which many other traits spring: a Wacko's image is everything, and therefore, he or she can do no wrong—or, at least, can't admit to it.

All levels of Wackos want the world to think they are always in the right. They will spend their entire lives perfecting and preserving this ideal image. Wackos will always find ways to clean up any trouble they may have gotten themselves into, and they won't hesitate to involve an innocent bystander in their first-class plan to get out of their jam. They will feel no remorse or guilt. And they will carry these secrets to their graves.

The earliest Wacko level often begins revealing its troubled self during adolescence. A burgeoning Wacko's first victim is almost always an unsuspecting younger sibling, as is the case with my former high school pal, Steven, and his older brother, Michael.

Who better to belittle, berate and psychologically torture than a younger sibling who can't leave for greener pastures? I would say that Michael was definitely a W1 by age sixteen. Steven's psyche succumbed to the persistent badgering, and he wilted into an accidental host by the time he was fourteen. Michael had himself a living, breathing, crying, moaning punching bag, and if there's one thing that Wackos love, it's getting a reaction. It was not unusual for Michael to disparage Steven's athletic ability, academic ability and just plain like-ability throughout their adolescence. The boys' bickering was chalked up to a normal case of sibling rivalry by those on the outside looking in.

When siblings are close in age, some competition is natural, but some sibs take it one step further. Michael was the older brother, but he had fumbled his way through life with clumsy social skills and an immature sensibility. Steven, on the other hand, made friends easily and was inherently well-mannered. It became Michael's mission in life to create the illusion that he, too, was coasting through adolescence with ease.

In true Wacko fashion, Michael had everyone fooled: his parents, his relatives, his teachers, his friends at school—you name it. Michael could do no wrong—or at least that's what he wanted people to think.

Michael left a cigarette in his shirt pocket once, and his mother found it when she was doing laundry. After school that day, she informed Michael of her discovery but said she would "wait until their father got home" to deal with it.

Michael knew what he needed to do: he needed to "shift the spotlight." While Steven was innocently practicing his soccer skills in the backyard, Michael was cooking up a way to make Steven look guilty—of something.

Physically, Steven was no match for Michael in the "cage match" sense of the word. Steven was certainly more athletic, but Michael fought dirty. When it came to verbal fisticuffs, however; it was Steven who could deliver the knock-out punch. Therein lay the solution for Michael: get Steven talking and let him blow his horn as loudly as he liked. Then, throw it all back in Steven's face.

Michael strolled authoritatively across their backyard, where Steven was practicing. With a look of complete disdain, Michael told Steven he was an insult to the sport. He calmly taunted, teased and ridiculed and didn't let up despite Steven's attempts to ignore him. Finally, Steven snapped and called Michael every name in the book—names I cannot repeat in *this* book. Steven's pent up power exploded, and he verbally attacked his older brother until his throat was raw.

When Michael was satisfied that he had heard enough, he casually turned away from his brother and strutted back toward the house, snickering under his breath.

That evening at the dinner table, Michael sat quietly and waited for his mother to drop the bomb. After she finished sharing the cigarette story, their father looked at Michael with a look of utter shock. Before he could express his disappointment, however; Michael spat, "Oh, if you think that's bad; you should hear this!" Like a scene from a movie, Michael pulled a small tape recorder out of his shirt pocket and pressed "play."

The whole family was treated to a colorful commentary. Every Technicolor cuss word that had spilled out of Steven's foul mouth had been recorded for posterity. What had conveniently *not* been recorded was the sneering sarcasm with which Michael had insulted his brother just moments before the "record" button was pressed. Or Michael calling Steven "Stephanie" like he always did to turn his younger brother beet-red with anger.

All eyes turned to Steven, whose face was now a ghostly shade of pale. With a look of disgust and disbelief, their father led Steven away from the table by his ear. Steven was grounded for a week and had to finish his meal in the bathroom. After all, that is "where pigs eat."

By the time the dust from Steven's outburst had settled, the story about Michael's cigarette elicited little interest. Michael got a verbal reprimand from his father and had to promise to lay off the smokes.

In no time at all, Michael was back on his high shelf, flawless and polished like a new trophy. Wackos always seem to know which buttons to push to shift the negative attention where they want it, and a W1 is an expert at covering his or her inappropriate tracks.

I lost touch with Michael and Steven after we graduated from high school, but there's no doubt in my mind that Michael's behavior continued into adulthood. If he ever screws up on the job, he will use whatever it takes to divert attention, I'm certain of it.

With a W1, working to maintain a perfect image is compulsory. They will do anything to protect that.

Which leads me back to a story about my friend, Suzanne, and her W1 sister, Sarah.

I love sharing the Suzanne stories simply because I know so many men and women can relate to the sordid tales about her wicked sibling.

Sarah epitomizes the "I do no wrong" trait. She and Suzanne were about as different as stinky English stilton and smooth cheddar. Sarah's Wacko behavior, which also included a sharp tongue and an inability to offer affection (which you will read more about later), didn't subside even after the two sisters no longer shared a home.

She and Suzanne were about as different as stinky English stilton and smooth cheddar.

Suzanne was an attractive, fun-loving senior in college with her future still an adventure to discover. Sarah was an average looking college graduate, working at a less-than-fulfilling job. Sarah's dissatisfaction with her own accomplishments hung around her neck like a twenty-pound albatross. Her perennial favorite target: younger sister, Suzanne.

The holiday season was in full swing, so not only was it time for eggnog and fruitcake, but also it was time for a heaping helping of bickering sisters.

Suzanne had been home from college for just a few days. Artistic since virtually day-one, it had become a tradition for Suzanne to decorate the house for the holidays, so she dove in joyfully. She decked the halls and walls with fresh pine, satin ribbons and hand blown German ornaments. Suzanne was savoring this time with her brother and parents until ... her sister came home.

Sarah was polite and quite charming for the first few days, which of course, surprised Suzanne. Bee-bopping into her room to get dressed for Christmas dinner, Suzanne found a shirt of hers lying crumpled on the floor. Immediately, she knew that Sarah had to be responsible. She recalled the times when she had wanted so desperately to borrow a shirt of Sarah's when they were growing up.

"Did you wear that shirt of mine?" Her sister would say to her when they were kids. "Well, put it back on a hanger and put it right back where you found it!"

Sarah would continue with her lips pursed in contempt. Her sharp tongue was always ready for action. It didn't matter that it was a shirt that Sarah no longer wore; she wasn't about to let Suzanne derive any pleasure from wearing it.

Now, as Suzanne stared at the wrinkled shirt, she struggled to contain the anger and hatred she felt toward her sister. Having just completed a seminar on self-empowerment, Suzanne turned on her heels and walked calmly into her sister's room. Literally feeling lightheaded from the suppressed rage inside her, she looked at her sister and calmly asked her if she wore the shirt that was thrown on her floor. Part of Suzanne couldn't believe she was even having this conversation with a grown woman.

Sarah looked Suzanne right in the eyes and smiled. She replied with a smooth, "Uhhhh huuuh." That was all Suzanne needed for her fury and resentment to reach the boiling point. Not only did Suzanne earn the $500 for the seminar by cleaning very dirty houses, but she also spent most of the time standing up in front of two hundred people discussing her antipathy toward her sister. She was about to make sure that was money and time well spent!

Suzanne went into her room, picked the shirt up off the floor and approached the object of her deflection in the hallway. Sarah was about to go downstairs to enjoy the rest of her day when she heard Suzanne yell, "I want you to wash the shirt, iron it and put it back on a hanger where you found it!"

Suzanne needed an ice pack to cool the heat rising from her face.

"Pooor little babyyy," Sarah snipped, whipping her hair around as she spun away.

With all the power Suzanne had, she took the shirt, moved ahead of Sarah and then turned to slam it into Sarah's face. Accustomed to winning every physical fight they had ever had since they were preschoolers, Sarah felt like she had been hit in the face by the boom of a boat as the captain tacked in a sixty-knot wind. But it didn't stop Sarah. Like all the bad seeds in horror movies, she got back up seemingly unaffected and went after Suzanne with a vengeance.

Suzanne's knee-jerk reaction was to slap Sarah across the face in self-defense.

"I hate you, you bitch!" Suzanne screamed, shocked at her own ability to lash out. The adrenalin was flowing.

Sarah went for the hair and began to pull with all of her might.

"Oh, you want to go there? Fine with me," Suzanne shouted at the top of her lungs as she grabbed a hunk of Sarah's hair. It was the one attribute they shared: a healthy outcropping of brown hair, and they each tried willfully to thin the other's locks with bare hands. Sarah had the advantage of having a lower center of gravity, as she was, to put it politely, built on a solid foundation. But Suzanne had the advantage of height and longer arms.

"Oh, you want to go there? Fine with me," Suzanne shouted at the top of her lungs as she grabbed a hunk of Sarah's hair.

Before they knew it, their mother was trying to separate them.

"Stop it now!" she screamed.

They went into their respective corners short of breath, but Suzanne knew she had won the round. She had thrown Sarah off balance, and that's exactly what she wanted to do. Wackos *hate* to lose their balance.

They went into their own rooms to cool off. Suzanne was looking at herself in her bathroom mirror laughing herself silly and flexing her muscles. She imagined she was on stage after the final act of a Broadway show and bowed to herself many times in the mirror. "Throw me the roses!" she whispered to her reflection while laughing.

Meanwhile, in Sarah's room, she cried on their mother's shoulder and told her she wanted to go home. She could really turn on the waterworks when she needed.

Their mother went into Suzanne's room and looked at her with resentment as she spoke in a low fuming tone, "Do You realize how much you upset your sister? She wants to leave right now and drive back home!"

"**Good**," Suzanne yelled over her mother's head while looking at Sarah's closed door. "**Go Home! I Can't Stand you!**"

And there you have it: another holiday with Suzanne and Sarah.

The sad thing about this story was that Suzanne wasted precious energy and time. In the end, their mother took Sarah's side because W1s are masterful at making themselves look right and the others wrong. Suzanne may have won that psychological battle with her sister, but a W1 will always be ready for another fight as long as you are willing to be in her life. Because Suzanne couldn't escape being around her difficult sister during the holidays, she should have ignored the shirt incident. That's where the real power comes in. Dismiss, dismiss, dismiss is my motto and is one you should remember and practice.

Sarah loved pushing Suzanne's buttons and that is exactly what she did with the shirt. Granted, she didn't get the reaction she was expecting.

This story reminded me of when I was growing up. We had a dog that was brutally attacked by the German shepherd next door. Our poor dog spent months recovering as he watched the neighbor's dog walk back and forth in front of our house. Banner would literally shake all over and stare right back at the brooding shepherd. Then, one day when my father was out front raking leaves, Banner got out and pounced on the German shepherd. Their fighting was vicious, and Banner's rage was not going to subside until the shepherd was dead. My father and the shepherd's owner beat the dogs with shovels to break them apart, but that did not deter Banner. Once Banner had the shepherd on his back, he delivered the coup de grâce, sinking his large white teeth deeply into the shepherd's neck. Then he got up and walked away. This is how I imagine Sarah was feeling at the time—mortally wounded. Absent death, however, a W1 will adjust her tactics and know how to push your buttons again—only in a different way. So know that and beware.

If you have a Wacko sibling, it's tough to avoid clashes during the holidays. The best you can do is keep your distance. Stay at a hotel, and do anything necessary to avoid contact with the Wacko. Protect yourself. And by all means, dismiss, dismiss, dismiss.

Tattletale, Tattletale

When a W1 needs a superiority fix or her image is in jeopardy, she loves to—no, *needs* to—tattle on someone. Tattling doesn't originate as a premeditated and vengeful act. It's a perfectly natural, innocent exercise performed hundreds of times a day by every five-year-old. What transforms this pedestrian practice into all-out Wacko warfare is when it is used by an insecure, bitter Wacko to boost his or her own self-worth.

This is another trait that obviously starts developing early in a person's life.

An easy-to-relate-to example of this would be the "office tattler," like Katrina whom I mentioned earlier. There's one in every office. He or she habitually bogs down the boss's time with blow-by-blow reports of which employees are making personal phone calls, using the copier for their kids' school projects and shopping online. For whatever reason, these Wacko tattlers feel compelled to point out each and every transgression of those around them. It's annoying, and it can force the boss to make an awkward choice: *Do I reprimand the tattler or the employee faxing personal paperwork?* The nerve-wracking outcome of the office tattler's tongue-wagging is that sometimes this strategy actually *works* and an otherwise model employee gets a black mark on her record for merely making a phone call to schedule a doctor's appointment.

Other chronic tattlers include siblings who never outgrow this nasty habit and continue to "tattle" well into adulthood. (Is it even *called* tattling after elementary school?) All they need are signs on their backs saying, "Look at me. I've always been and always will be the good child." I'm not saying that potentially dangerous behavior, like drug use, should go unreported. I'm talking about opportunistic, acidic Wacko siblings who jump on every superficial slip-up to chisel away at a fellow sibling's solid reputation.

You may have found yourself the intended target of this grown-up form of tattling, or you may have witnessed others having to fend off these attacks. Either way, this would be a good place to remind you to watch, look and listen. If there are people in your life who derive way too much pleasure from reporting the miscues of others, consider them to be tattlers and be on the lookout for other Wacko behavior so you can properly classify them.

Just know that a W1 will tattle on anyone, at any age, if she thinks it will make her look superior. If you simply listen, you will hear these people—young and old—all around you.

I'll Cut You with My Tongue

If you're beginning to think that W1s love to brandish their verbal power to make them appear dominant, you're absolutely correct. What they lack in personal power they try to overcompensate for by using their mouths as weapons of mass destruction.

For some maturing Wackos, tattling eventually loses its luster, and in its place, a more direct form of verbal assault will arise. Rather than tattle to the nearest authority figure, W1s may develop a tendency to blurt out insults, freely spread gossip and, in general, spew whatever garbage is piling up in their minds.

If you're ever a target, a Wacko's tongue will slice you like a knife through butter. When Maureen sneered that I was "just a housewife," she cut my soul in two. Her tone screamed disrespect; it was clear she regarded me as inferior.

What they can't accomplish through face-to-face inter-action, Wackos will carry out behind someone's back

---

Wackos generally appear calm and in control; after all, they have an image to uphold. But don't underestimate what is simmering beneath the surface. If casually or blatantly criticized, a Wacko won't hesitate to use his or her sharp tongue to lash the nearest person. A wave of the harshest words will burst from the Wacko's mouth without pause. Most of us walk away from a confrontation saying to ourselves, "I wish I would have said this" or "I wish I would have thought of that." A W1 will immediately snap out an astonishing, destructive response perfectly tailored for the situation. It will happen so quickly that the shock will render you incapable of defending yourself. It'll make you wonder if the Wacko uses spare time to conceive and rehearse shocking comebacks. This behavior can be traced back to a Wacko's need to uphold the "perfect" image. Any perceived insult threatens to tarnish the image that the Wacko will do anything to protect.

What they can't accomplish through face-to-face interaction, Wackos will carry out behind someone's back in the form of gossip and rumors. Don't think for one minute that they won't make up stories if they have to.

How do you identify Wackos early on to protect yourself from emotional destruction? It's as simple as flipping a burger. Watch, look and listen to what people say about others. If they gossip about their friend's vital stuff, they will talk about yours. Once again; you will never be the exception. Never share private information with a Wacko unless you want your darkest secrets to have a starring role in teatime conversations all over town.

I Can't Offer Affection

W1s actually desire affection, but they don't know how to give it.

When I was a young girl, I went away to Girl Scout camp. In our cabin was a group of third- and fourth-graders, some of whom were sisters—including my friend, Suzanne and her older sister, Sarah. One night at about 10 P.M., we started hearing animal noises outside our cabin. All of the third-graders started screaming, and like a corps of well-trained den mothers, the fourth-graders pulled back their blankets and beckoned their little sisters and campers into their protective arms. The older girls felt like leaders and the younger ones felt protected. Only Sarah with her emotionless expression and cold demeanor refused to allow her younger sister into her bed. All of the other campers urged Sarah to "lighten up," but it didn't make a dent it her armor. I can still see the vacant look in Sarah's eyes and the downcast humiliation in Suzanne's. We all bickered with our siblings from time to time, but we still loved each other. Poor Suzanne. She was so eager for any form of affection that Sarah was willing to give, but she found herself rejected yet again. The rest of us looked on in disgust. No amount of coaxing could get the frosty sister to change her mind, even when the campers started calling her names. In the end, one of the older girls let Suzanne crawl into her bed, and three campers tried to sleep in a twin bunk. Suzanne spent the rest of the trip propping her chin up. She wasn't as devastated as most children would have been because she had never experienced any love from her sister, ever. How can you miss what you have never had? Offering comfort and affection to her younger sister was something that Sarah could not physically bring herself to do. One night around the campfire, Sarah sat alone because she refused to sit with her arm around Suzanne like the other campers were doing with their little sisters and Scout sisters. Suzanne found comfort with some of the other campers, but the one person she wanted affection from remained distant.

My guess would be that W1s start developing this trait very early on as a defense mechanism to give the impression that affection is not important to them. If a W1 ever reaches out to you with a hug, just know how much effort this simple gesture requires. Don't take it personally when it only lasts a nano-second before the patronizing back-patting begins and the Wacko pushes you away. And, don't take it personally if the physical contact comes with numerous strings attached. You'll get a clear example of this after reading Chapter 7.

I'm Antisocial

For W1s, fantasy and escape are the drugs of choice. Some people escape reality by drinking too much booze, but a W1 has the remarkable ability to shut out the world without disrupting his or her body chemistry. A Wacko entrenched in a book or crossword puzzle wouldn't know if there was an earthquake. In the midst of a chaotic family reunion, office gathering or holiday celebration, an uncomfortable Wacko might choose to talk on her cell phone endlessly, or she might maintain an unnatural interest in a coffee table book. Interacting with others in a situation that is not carefully scripted scares the hell out of this type because it puts her at risk of having her weaknesses exposed. Wackos would rather do anything than talk about or share feelings in any form.

While working part-time in a department store during college, I met and became friends with another young woman who also worked there. We attended separate colleges, but we were at similar stages in our lives and we bonded quickly. We took advantage of our employee discounts and shopped together after our shift. It became immediately clear to me that Patricia was very worldly and well-educated. When she spoke, her voice was clear and confident. She seemed to know a lot about a wide range of topics, had been to a lot of different cities and had well-formed opinions regarding current affairs. I found myself getting tongue-tied around her and growing increasingly self-conscious of my word choices and grammar. She seemed older than her years, as if she'd been living on her own since she was ten. I would soon find out that there was some truth to that.

As I got to know Patricia, I learned that her mother was a celebrated actress of both the stage and the big screen, which explained Patricia's travel history. Before long, I found myself backstage with Patricia at various New York theaters and surrounded by famous people at her mother's lavish parties.

Any young adult would have been swept away by the excitement and the intrigue of floating in a sea of celebrities, and I was no exception. Had I been paying closer attention to Patricia's actions at the time instead of staring at the acting-world elite, I would have realized that Patricia herself wasn't exactly surrounded by a posse of close friends. In fact; she was shadowed by a posse of exactly one: me. At the time, I didn't question her relative isolation; I was just glad that she had befriended me.

In retrospect, our friendship was reasonably one-sided. She once tried to turn off a new boyfriend of mine by calling him and telling him that I was older than he was.

"So, Christina is older than me?" my former beau asked Patricia.

"I think you mean 'older than I,'" Patricia corrected him.

I chalked it up to petty jealousy and decided to cut her some slack. After all, I was balancing a busy social life and she was balancing ... well ... me.

She would teeter back and forth between inviting me to parties and trying to tick me off. I seriously considered ending our friendship once while visiting her at college. We got separated at a party, and when I returned to her apartment, she refused to answer the door. I knocked and pounded on the door for several hours until I finally gave up. Cold and tired, I laid down on the front stoop and used her disintegrating rubber doormat as a blanket. Hey, when you're in Ithaca, New York, in October you do what you have to do! In the morning, she opened the door with a smile on her face. Her teeth were all exactly the same size, which I always thought was kind of strange.

"Why the hell didn't you answer the damn door, Patricia?" I fumed.

She replied indifferently, "Maybe you just didn't knock loudly enough," and turned her back to me as she walked away.

Her behavior confused the tar out of me, but I hadn't seen the worst of it, yet.

I suppose I stuck around so long because I felt sorry for her. It had to have been difficult for Patricia to have a mother who was always surrounded by admirers, hailed for her physical beauty and charisma. Not that Patricia was ugly—her face was pleasant enough—she was just plain by comparison. A bouquet of carnations can certainly be beautiful, but there's a reason why they don't cost as much as roses. If Patricia minded being more of the "carnation" variety, she certainly didn't let on. In fact, her unruly brown hair seemed purposely unkempt, as if having "bad hair" was her way of rebelling against a mother who was always pristinely coifed. Patricia's hair was a fusion of wiry brown tendrils springing haphazardly from clumps that resembled steel wool, and she made no effort to tame it that I had ever witnessed. Her mother's physical appearance coupled with her physical absence most of the time made for a lonely upbringing, I'm sure. I wanted so much to be a friend to Patricia because it was clear to me that she really needed one.

Then one summer, Patricia invited me to accompany her on her annual trip to Hawaii to visit her father, who lived there. Spend two months in Hawaii? I packed my bags faster than you can say "poi!" Not only would this trip prove to be a learning experience for me in the cultural sense, but also it was my earliest experience with the aforementioned two-by-four. After two months with Patricia, the board was going to smack me hard—at roughly 36,000 feet.

All I can say is, I'm glad that I enjoy my own company because I was about to spend ten hours with my own thoughts. We boarded the plane and I was giddy with fantasies about the islands: white sandy beaches ... good looking guys ... luaus.... Two months of paradise. When I turned to talk to Patricia, my smile fell to the floor. Her head was buried deeply in a book. She didn't seem to notice that I was there. Patricia was quite well-traveled, so I suppose the trip to Hawaii was merely an annual habit for her. She was going through the motions, and I was simply the passenger in the seat beside her. With all of the enthusiasm I could channel I asked her to describe her father's house on Diamond Head. "It's OK," she muttered without looking up from her book. Those were the only two words she spoke to me. I was reduced to talking to the three-year-old sitting next to me. It was slowly beginning to sink in to my brain that the reason why I was Patricia's only friend was because I was the only one lacking the chutzpah to simply walk away.

I'm glad that I enjoy my own company because I was about to spend ten hours with my own thoughts.

Her rude, antisocial behavior ebbed and flowed like the Pacific shoreline throughout our vacation. She would take me to parties, then leave me on my own. She would tell me about her "friends" and cousins who lived on the island, but she would never introduce me to any of them. I felt like a high school misfit who got invited to the prom only because my date didn't want to walk into the dance alone.

I realized that this vacation was going to be a sink or swim experience, and swim I did! I socialized with her cousins whenever possible and discovered that they could barely tolerate Patricia. Spending time with her father was interesting as well. He was a deeply religious man and made every effort to convert me into a missionary, but at least I wasn't alone.

Toward the end of the trip, I decided to give my tan one final boost by slathering myself with baby oil. Having never been in Hawaii before, I had little, if any, appreciation for the strength of the sun's rays. Patricia, naturally, failed to warn me of the consequences of my foolishness. The next morning, Patricia's father didn't know whether he should fly me to a leper colony or to a hospital! I received absolutely zero sympathy from Wacko.

Two months later, after surviving the summer with Patricia, I had been hit by the two-by-four. I was done. I looked over at her during the return trip to New York and wondered where the three-year-old was when I needed him. A lock of Patricia's itchy hair kept snaking its way into my nostril, and I would have gladly handed the toddler a pair of scissors. Reading her book for another ten hours was the salt in the wound.

After we were back in college, I shoved my Mother Teresa leanings aside and wrote her a letter explaining my feelings about her ill treatment. She returned the letter to me with corrections made to my spelling and grammar but no apologies for the way she treated me. Can you guess why she invited me to go on vacation with her? Because she needed a friend in tow to create the illusion that she was capable of having friends. Of course, when I was nineteen, I hadn't met my therapist yet, so I hadn't been taught to *watch, look and listen*. If I had, I never would have gone on the trip.

Looking back, Patricia embodied every W1 trait and wore them on her sleeve 24/7. She could *do no wrong* and therefore the essence of the letter I wrote to her after our trip fell on deaf ears. She was a *tattletale* when she called my boyfriend in the hopes of shocking him with my real age; she freely *brandished her sharp tongue* after I'd spent the night on a cement stoop. She certainly couldn't give me (or anyone else it seemed) an ounce of *affection,* even when I'd sizzled myself like a piece of bacon in Hawaii. She was *antisocial* on our trip to Hawaii and off and on throughout our friendship.

Patricia called me several months later and invited me to go on a cruise with her and her mother. The prospect of enjoying a cruise surrounded by celebrities was tempting, but I said "no." I didn't need to rub elbows with the rich and famous to validate my own self-worth. That was almost the last time I heard from her. Several years later, she tracked me down through some mutual acquaintances and asked if we could resume the relationship. I listened to the things she was saying on the other line. "Once again, you have what I want. You have a husband and a family, and I have no one," she said. My assumptions about her loneliness proved true, but that didn't excuse the way she had treated me. What I heard was jealousy and trouble ahead if I let her into my world. That was too high a price for me.

When I was in college, I took Patricia's behavior personally. I'm telling you now that you can't take this kind of Wacko personally when you are on the receiving end. It's not about you.

Chapter

7 Don't Let Your Guard Down

Don't underestimate the negative impact that a W1 can have on your life with just words and antisocial behavior. Those who are confident and self-assured can probably tolerate a W1 and experience few, if any, ill effects. If you are a host, however, letting your guard down around a W1 would be like leaning over a gas stove with long hair. Expect it to catch on fire.

The last time Suzanne let her guard down with her Wacko sister, Sarah was about ten years ago, when they were both in their thirties. Sarah invited Suzanne and her family to stay at her house for a few days—a gesture completely out of character for Sarah. But she made a convincing argument, assuring Suzanne how much fun they were going to have together. Even though "love me, accept me" Suzanne was in therapy at the time and knew better than to trust Sarah under any circumstances, she pushed aside her initial reservations and graciously accepted the invitation. Once Suzanne and her family arrived, Sarah was unusually kind and, at one point, put her arm around Suzanne. (Red flag! Remember what I said about shows of affection?) When they were kids, their parents would make Sarah stand still so Suzanne could kiss her on the cheek and say good night. Sarah would comply, her body stiff as a board, just to appease their parents. Now, Sarah was freely giving affection for the first time in thirty years? That night, an enthusiastic Suzanne said to her husband, "I think we have had a breakthrough in our relationship. She has never been this nice to me. Maybe now she has finally gotten over her petty jealousies with me." Her husband's response was a cautious, "Uh huh."

The next day, Sarah was hosting a barbecue, and Suzanne helped her sister prepare food for the event. Suzanne left to get dressed for the gathering as Sarah remained in the kitchen finishing up the final food preparation. When Sarah saw Suzanne walk out of the guest room wearing a silk dress and earrings, her hair pulled up in a French twist, the claws came out. Sarah's right eye twitched anxiously. An additional fifty pounds had attached itself to her frame, and she had draped her body in an oversized t-shirt that hung halfway to her thighs. The vastness of their physical divide had never been as pronounced as it was that day.

The sisters were alone in the kitchen, and Sarah saw the perfect opportunity to attack. As Suzanne walked over to the kitchen counter with her heart wide open, thanking God for giving her back her sister, Sarah went in for the kill using words. At least hair-pulling had been yanked from the day's menu.

She leaned over the kitchen counter and stuck her face close to Suzanne's. Sarah's freshly bleached mustache glistened in the sunlight that shone through the kitchen windows.

"Look at you! This is a barbecue, and you are in a silk dress. Look at your hair! Who do you think you are? Ivana Trump?!" Suzanne stood there calmly and quietly as her sister verbally attacked everything about her. A tiny voice warned Suzanne that this was exactly what Sarah had wanted all along: a prime opportunity to pounce on Suzanne's feelings once more. "No wonder nobody likes you. You are so superficial," Sarah ranted, releasing her own personal nuclear bomb upon the one person who certainly didn't deserve it. Suzanne suddenly found herself back in the cabin at Girl Scout camp: she would never be loved by her sister no matter how hard she tried. There was just one major difference this time around: Suzanne could leave.

Suzanne looked at Sarah calmly. "I'm sorry you feel that way about me," Suzanne said, wiping the spit from her face. "I wear my hair like this because I think it's cool and fun and, as you know, I have always loved beautiful clothes. As for my friends, they love me just the way I am." Suzanne spoke with sincerity and without judgment or anger. What she really wanted to say was, *You bleached your mustache, but you forgot to do something about those nostril hairs,* but that would have been stooping to Sarah's level. Instead, Suzanne calmly walked back to the bedroom, cried, pulled herself together and went back out by the pool in a pair of tattered jeans.

Shortly after their less-than-loving sisterly exchange, Suzanne whispered in her husband's ear, "We are leaving in the morning."

Shortly after their less-than-loving sisterly exchange, Suzanne whispered in her husband's ear, "We are leaving in the morning." Her husband took one look at her eyes and could tell she had been crying. He put his arms around her defeated shoulders and nuzzled his face close to her ear. "What happened?" He whispered.

"We'll talk about it later," she said, gulping down a wave of tears and fixing a brave smile on her face.

After crying for the entire twelve-hour ride home, Suzanne knew she had been hit by the two-by-four, splinters and all. It was just what she needed to have the courage to permanently end her relationship with Sarah. Several days later, Suzanne cried again as she relayed the story to her mother. Her mother's response was that Sarah hadn't said a thing about the confrontation when they had spoken earlier. Of course. Sarah was trying to cover her ample backside.

The lesson here is that if you have anyone in your life like Sarah, don't waste thirty-some years beating a dead horse. Forgive her, bless the lessons learned and "Dear John" the Wacko immediately. Suzanne tried her best, and for that, she has a clear conscience. Sarah may have viewed her sister as weak, but in fact, Suzanne was strong enough to survive her sister's abuse for all those years and eventually put it behind her.

Suzanne's story underscores the fact that Wackos never change, so you should never let your guard down. This is such an important lesson that I'm going to share another W1 story with you, just to really drive the point home. And besides, no respectable collection of Wacko tales would be complete without a wedding saga or two, and this book is no exception.

My friend Genevieve experienced first-hand the wrath of a W1 before, during and after her wedding day. I have to say, I think Genevieve handled the situation with more grace than I ever could have mustered.

If you've got an in-law who gives you nightmares, read on.

Henry couldn't wait to introduce his bride-to-be to his folks, and Genevieve was equally eager to meet the parents of the man with whom she had fallen madly in love. Hand in hand, they walked through the front door of Henry's childhood home, where his parents were hosting an engagement party. It was Genevieve's maiden voyage to the home Henry had grown up in, and she quietly took it all in. What she saw made it abundantly clear why Henry now had such a fondness for minimalist-style décor. His parents' foyer was virtually wallpapered with portrait after portrait of Henry and his parents at various stages in their lives. Lining the hallway was a mismatched array of accent tables topped with yet more photos, porcelain collectibles and what Genevieve supposed were antique candlesticks, although they simply looked old and dingy to her.

Henry's parents greeted them graciously, and then Henry and his father headed for the living room to join the party. Genevieve looked hopefully at her future mother-in-law, who was lifting one of the photos from a nearby demilune. The temperature in the foyer was about to dip.

Wanda squinted cynically at the photograph in her hands. "You look fat in this picture," she purred like Betty Davis to her future daughter-in-law, batting her clumpy, mascara-laden eyelashes. Wanda had an irritating habit of drawing out her words to make whatever she said—no matter how pointless—sound overly dramatic. The photo in question was one that Henry had taken of Genevieve in front of a museum they had recently visited. At just over 5' 8", Genevieve tipped the scales at a scant 118 pounds. She couldn't have looked fat if she'd wanted to.

Wanda calmly ran her bony fingers through her thinning hair and looked at Genevieve with wide-open eyes for a response. Shocked, Genevieve quietly asked where the bathroom was. Wanda pointed the way with a satisfied smirk. Genevieve was forced to employ the "run to the bathroom, cry and pull yourself together" routine within minutes of meeting Wanda.

Being a classic W1, Wanda used her words to belittle Genevieve, careful to make this hurtful comment when no one else was listening. Everyone else was cheerfully and genuinely celebrating Henry and Genevieve's engagement.

Wanda didn't waste any time making it perfectly clear that she wasn't celebrating.

After the exceedingly sensitive, walking, breathing guest returned from the bathroom, she planted a smile on her face and steeled herself for round two. The last thing she wanted was to spoil Henry's visit with his family by getting too upset over Wanda's comment.

Wanda was used to being the Queen Bee, so it took just a few "what a beautiful couple" comments to send Wanda over the edge.

The irony of Wanda's remark was that Genevieve had battled mild anorexia for years. She had never been hospitalized, but had come damned close. Wanda seemed to sense Genevieve's insecurity over her body image and knew exactly which buttons to push. Genevieve stuck close to her fiancé for the remainder of the engagement party. They were a striking couple—Henry with his charming, chiseled features and raven hair, and Genevieve with her long, sleek honey-colored hair that complemented the long lines of her slender body. Wanda was used to being the Queen Bee, so it took just a few "what a beautiful couple" comments from the well-wishers at the party to send Wanda over the edge. It became her mission in life to regain her ranking as "the one most deserving of attention."

For fifteen years, Genevieve's signature statement would be, "Your mother doesn't like me." Her tone always bordered on apologetic, as if she blamed herself.

And for fifteen years, Henry countered with "Don't be ridiculous. Besides, my old man adores you."

Up until then, Wanda's behavior bore on with Genevieve the target of sharp-tongued comments and uncivilized remarks right up until the day of the wedding. Wanda was careful to exude her nastiness when no one other than Genevieve was there to witness it. Not even the happiest of occasions could make Wanda change her tune. In fact, Wanda made it her personal mission to turn Henry's father against Genevieve as well, and she eventually succeeded. But it was Wanda who had honed her emotional abuse skills to a fine art.

About a month before the wedding, Wanda casually mentioned to Genevieve that she would be strutting down the aisle in a white lace dress at the wedding despite knowing it's customary for only the bride to wear white. What did my friend say to Wanda? Not a darn thing. At least the thought of Wanda in a white dress was enough to get Genevieve talking with Henry. Genevieve attempted to harness some of her personal power by letting her complaints fly, only to be told time and time again by Henry that she had to be mistaken about his mother. Poor Henry. He truly believed that his mother liked Genevieve because he had never witnessed the way Wanda emotionally and mentally battered his bride-to-be. Genevieve knew that until Henry witnessed the truth for himself, she was powerless. She had no choice but to plaster a smile on her face and make the most of what was supposed to be one of the happiest days in her life.

Being an all-forgiving queen of doormats, Genevieve took it upon herself to make excuses for her future mother-in-law's behavior to keep things running smoothly as the wedding day drew closer. Somehow, Henry's parents weaseled their way out of hosting the rehearsal dinner, so Genevieve's parents graciously held the dinner at their home. In true Wacko fashion, Wanda made an entrance that everyone would notice.

Wanda burst through the front door wearing every piece of jewelry that she owned. Her lipstick was thick and loud. Her pancake makeup had settled into the deep cracks surrounding her exaggerated features. She sauntered toward Genevieve, her hips swaying like a pendulum as if to say "Hey, everyone! I'm still sexy!" In a thunderous voice she asked, "I'm sorry, what is your mother's name?" Everyone turned around and stared at her in shock. Wanda undoubtedly thought that the guests were admiring her lavish beauty. Please. She looked like Telly Savalas in drag.

Wanda undoubtedly thought that the guests were admiring her lavish beauty. Please. She looked like Telly Savalas in drag.

Wanda spent the remainder of the rehearsal dinner flirting shamelessly with Genevieve's father. Genevieve's mother, a sophisticated lady, took it all in stride.

The wedding day came and went without incident. Wanda surely thought that she had outshined the bride, but Genevieve's beauty and poise lifted her above any controversy. Most guests recognized Wanda's behavior for what it was: a manifestation of her petty jealousy and just plain rudeness. It would take Henry a little bit longer to "see the light."

As the marriage progressed, Wanda's determination to break Genevieve's spirit kicked into high gear. She barreled ahead arrogantly, just like the Titanic. Her ego was the size of an iceberg, and it was about to shatter.

It was Thanksgiving Day, and Henry and Genevieve were thrilled to introduce their first child to the in-laws. Genevieve had never looked more beautiful—motherhood completely agreed with her. Genevieve, however, still battled her internal demons and struggled to ignore the few extra pounds that had been added to her frame. Her sensitivity was running high; she so hoped for a peaceful meal. The meal didn't turn out to be entirely peaceful, but it did prove to be an important turning point.

Wanda sat at the head of the table, seething with jealousy because she wasn't the center of attention. One by one, her claws started to pop out under the table.

"Henry Jr. seems so happy," Genevieve's sister-in-law said fondly.

"Well, I try to smile at him all the time and give him about a thousand kisses a day!" Genevieve gushed in high spirits.

Wanda narrowed her eyes like she always did before pouncing. She grabbed the seat of her chair as if to prevent her explosive anger from rocketing her to the moon. Her bony fingers were covered with every ring she owned, the appearance made even gaudier by her oversized fingernails. She growled in a low voice, dramatically drawing out certain words the way she always did, "And what do you think I did? Sat there and snarled at my children?"

Everyone at the table was momentarily stunned. Henry quickly resumed the conversation to cut the tension, but he'd finally witnessed what Genevieve had been enduring since the day she met Wanda.

When the furor died down, Genevieve silently rose from the table and retreated to her favorite place to cry: the bathroom. She would never feel accepted by Henry's family no matter what she said or did, she thought.

On the airplane ride home, Genevieve cried the entire way. After four years of enduring ill treatment by this woman and starting to get it from the father in-law, she had had about all she could take. Finally, Henry had to admit what he didn't want to: his mother really didn't like the woman he loved— his best friend, greatest supporter and mother of his child. Genevieve's spirits lifted; her husband was finally on her side in this particular matter. He called home and spoke with his father, asking him to reason with Wanda so that Henry and Genevieve could salvage some sort of relationship with Henry's folks. Henry's call was in vain.

Genevieve and Henry eventually welcomed another child into their loving family, but Henry's parents made no secret of the fact that they didn't care for the child's name. They even refused to call their granddaughter by her given name. Things had finally reached a crescendo, and Henry got whacked in the head with the same two-by-four that had sent Genevieve reeling before their wedding.

Henry severed all contact with his parents, and it was just what Genevieve needed. No more listening to Wanda's laments that Genevieve's boobs were too small, her hips were too wide or that she needed to put highlights in her hair. No more listening to family gossip that Genevieve didn't do anything and that Henry took care of the kids and did the grocery shopping and the laundry in addition to working virtually nonstop at the business he owned. The assertion was ludicrous, but it bothered Genevieve just the same.

The couples kept their distance for two years. Then, Henry decided it was time to offer an olive branch. He thought that in time his mother would change her ways. Obviously, this book wasn't available for him to read yet, or he wouldn't have made such a foolish gesture. He called his parents to attempt to make things right.

Genevieve was supportive of Henry's attempt to reconcile with his folks, and she jumped back in with both feet to help make things magnificent. It was hurricane season once again, but this time, the kids were going to get caught in the eye of the storm.

When Henry and Genevieve needed to go on a business trip, Henry's folks were first in line to watch the two children. Genevieve warily accepted their offer to baby-sit, and Henry gave them instructions to not feed the children candy or dairy products. Genevieve knew full well that, had she made such a request, Henry's parents would have ignored her. Little did she know, Henry's parents would ignore *his* request because they still assumed that it was Genevieve calling all the shots.

Henry and Genevieve had hardly backed their car out of the driveway when Wanda went to town with the old man right by her side. "Isn't it horrible that your mother doesn't let you have candy? Your poor father is being forced to eat health food! Here, have some milk, ice cream and candy. Your mother isn't around!" It didn't end there, either. Both Wanda and her husband insulted Genevieve in front of the children for the rest of their stay.

When Henry and Genevieve returned, their children begged to never be left with their grandparents again, and it remains that way today.

Genevieve got hit with the wood square in the chops this time. She tasted the blood in her mouth and sent the clothes to the dry cleaner. The deal was done. She let her guard down because Wanda pretended to care. What a performance the wannabe actress gave.

The next time Genevieve and Henry dined with his parents, Genevieve was ready for anything Wanda dished out. Wanda had crossed the line by not caring for the children the way she had been instructed. Like a lioness guarding her cubs, Genevieve was on high alert.

During dinner, Wanda flashed Genevieve a huge fake smile as she purred, "When do you think I can have the children over again?" She batted her eyelashes and smiled broadly, which emphasized her enormous front teeth that had a bad "fill in the space" job.

Genevieve smiled and replied calmly, "Well, you are welcome to spend time with the children when you can stop putting me down in front of them. My children love me and when you do that, it makes them feel uncomfortable." Genevieve had finally taken control.

"What! I've done no such thing," she said blinking, trying to separate the clumps of mascara that virtually glued her eyes shut.

"Oh, I'm sorry, but yes you did," Genevieve replied firmly and with genuine pity on her face. The children never had an unsupervised visit with Henry's parents again.

It took Genevieve fifteen years to finally acknowledge that she would never be accepted by her in-laws. If her mother-in-law didn't have any respect for her from the beginning, why would it change over the years? That one simple admission set Genevieve free. It wasn't her stuff; it was Wanda's. Wanda had a razor-sharp tongue; was incapable of showing affection; never admitted to doing anything wrong; and was masterful enough to turn the father-in-law against Genevieve as a cover. Wanda used her Wacko ways to bring herself up and drag a young and insecure bride down. To this day, Wanda has no real friends.

Genevieve finally realized who and what she was dealing with. If you can relate to Genevieve, do what she did but don't wait fifteen years.

It took Genevieve fifteen years to finally acknowledge that she would never be accepted by her in-laws.

Henry tried to maintain a relationship with his parents. Genevieve dealt with it by making herself scarce when the in-laws arrived for a visit. Of course, her absence just gave them another reason to detest her and to gossip. They would always look for something. When Genevieve had to be around them she remained quiet and avoided any exchange of information other than superficial chatter.

Genevieve's story is a lengthy one, but it's replete with valuable lessons. There are plenty of things that Genevieve could have done differently to shorten her exposure to the Wacko in her life. As you read the stories in this book, think to yourself how the Wackos could have been handled another way. Performing this exercise will help you understand, and learn to apply, the information contained between these covers.

Here are some of the lessons to be learned by Genevieve's struggles with her mother-in-law:

- ▶ Genevieve should have told Wanda that she would not be welcome at the wedding if she were going to wear a white lace dress. Period. There are some lines you simply don't cross, and if you do, you get tossed. This was one of them.

▶ Genevieve should have insisted upon Henry's support in this matter. There is power in numbers, and Henry needed to understand his obligation to do so. Husbands many times support their mothers over their wives. This will inevitably lead to conflict and possibly divorce. Boys, when you marry, your wife becomes No. 1. Moms, when your sons marry, he belongs to another. If you can't see it, then you're a Wacko in someone's life.

▶ When Wanda went overboard with her sarcasm at Thanksgiving dinner, Genevieve should have leaned over and whispered in Henry's ear, "Honey, I am leaving in the morning. If you would like to join me that would be great." Don't ever give a W1 the satisfaction of boiling over. Be a gentleman or a lady and leave with dignity. There is no disgrace in standing up for yourself, only in failing to do so when warranted.

▶ Pay the few extra bucks for Caller ID (if you haven't already) and never talk on the phone to someone who gives you bad vibes. Some people laugh off the concept of people giving off a certain "energy," but let me assure you that it's true. My husband got off the phone with an extremely negative person and his neck was so out of alignment the next day that he had to see a chiropractor. Don't put that energy against your ear. Always use the speaker phone function if you must communicate with such a person.

▶ When you see a Wacko in social situations, make the conversation short and sweet and then move on to someone else. If the Wacko thinks you are being rude, so be it. You aren't doing anything to abuse her like she would do to you if you stood there and spoke to her for hours on end. Furthermore, a Wacko really isn't interested in you or what you have to say in the first place. He or she is only looking for what she can use against you. Never, ever discuss personal and confidential information with a Wacko of any level. They will *always* use it against you.

▶ It doesn't matter that Wanda was insecure, had a bad childhood, was jealous of every woman who came into her house, etc. All that matters is how Genevieve wanted to be treated. The rest of it is Wanda's stuff. Genevieve shouldn't have tried to take it on.

▶ The in-laws will never know how much Genevieve and Henry love each other, how much they have been through together, what a fantastic mother Genevieve has been to their grandchildren and what a rock she is to their family. It's their loss.

▶ Henry is a religious man and believes in honoring his parents. Genevieve stays out of his way and lets him do just that—but without her. And that's OK.

▶ If you pay attention in the beginning, you will see what you will get in the end. Stay in a relationship with a Wacko and you will end up being pelted with your own personal Molotov cocktail.

W1s will do anything to uphold a pristine image; they will use their verbal skills to attack; they cannot easily show affection; and they are primarily antisocial. How you choose to relate, if at all, to a W1 is entirely up to you. Most of this behavior is not devastating if you are prepared for it and you know how to react or how not to react to it. That is the key. You should never take this behavior personally. Remember: it's not about you.

As Wacko
Behavior Broadens

By the time someone evolves into a Level 2 Wacko, he or she has fully mastered all of the beneficial W1 traits and started to tack on a few new ones. Perhaps for some Wackos, the W1 traits start to lose their effectiveness over time. Like someone with a chemical dependency, the Wacko must add new strategies to maintain the same heightened sense of power and control that she spends her life chasing.

But, as Wacko characteristics multiply, so do the ill effects on the Wackos themselves. With the early onset of W1 traits, we saw an increase in health problems and the challenges associated with the inability to sever the apron strings. The telltale sign that a Wacko has progressed to Level 2 is that, in addition to the earlier problems, a Wacko 2 (W2) starts losing friends at a rapid rate. In fact, I try to refrain from using the word "friend" when discussing a W2's relationships. Once a Wacko's behavior has reached Level 2, she has all but lost her capacity to be a true friend or to have a true friend. I'd ask a W2 if this was the intended result, but I doubt that I would get a straight answer.

It's the Wacko Way or the Highway

As Wacko behavior expands, any circle of friends will drastically contract, primarily because W2s can't relate amicably to anyone who does not share their every point of view. If you've ever encountered the type, you know how uncomfortable they can make everyday situations.

Imagine yourself sitting at a nice café having lunch, and the first time you disagree with the W2 sitting across from you, her expression freezes, and she stops chewing her food. You expect her to engage in a friendly debate, but instead, she only stares at you as if you've just run over her cat. From that point on, her demeanor turns frosty and you find yourself surrounded by her subzero aura. Another meal ruined.

Imagine yourself sitting at a nice café having lunch, and the first time you disagree with the person sitting across from you, she stops chewing her food.

When communicating with this type, expect your point of view to be wrong, your lifestyle to be wrong, the way you are raising your kids to be wrong and even the arrangement of your pots and pans to be wrong. Furthermore, W2s cannot mentally handle any real or perceived level of resistance.

If you choose to defend your position when a Wacko wages war, do so quickly and calmly—the fewer words, the better. My friend Jessica once told me that anything more than five words would satisfy a Wacko's need to be right. When you talk too much, Jessica theorized, you come off sounding defensive. This is one facet of what I call the "Jessica Method," which you'll learn more about soon. Through my experiences, I've also learned (the hard way) that talking too much can exacerbate the Wacko's contempt, and agreeing to disagree won't work, either. It's the Wacko way or the highway. Be the lady who *doesn't* protest too much, and move on to another topic.

W2s are still capable of interacting on a friendly basis, but don't be fooled. It's only temporary. A W2 will employ the "Aren't I nice?" act if she wants or needs something from someone. In the end, however, her insecurities, paranoia and defense mechanisms (which you will read about shortly) will surface. If witnessing the "Aren't I nice?" act turns your stomach, rest assured that it will be short-lived. The Wacko will give away his or her true barmy self in a matter of weeks or, at the most, in a matter of months. Use the watch, look and listen technique if you suspect that you've got a W2 in your life. If you can avoid W2s, I recommend doing so.

Virtually the only arrangement through which a W2 can sustain a long-term relationship is via long distance. Casual contacts from out-of-town and classmates from long ago come in handy for W2s. Smart Wackos hold in reserve a handful of acquaintances who have never witnessed the Wacko in full Wacko action. When the Wacko has been dumped by someone who's learned the truth and she needs an attention fix, she'll initiate contact with an out-of-towner. The Wacko may even suggest an overnight visit to give others the impression that she does indeed have close friends. Keeping the visit short and sweet is critical for the W2 because Wackos can't sustain the "nice" act for too long. I knew a W2 who made the mistake of hosting a "friend" for two weeks. By the time the houseguest departed, the W2 was squirming like her laxative had kicked in. For some strange reason, the Wacko's internal anxiety prompted her to mail a rude letter to her former guest, attempting to set her straight on some subjects that were gnawing away at the Wacko. She just had to get the last word in, and that was the end of that relationship.

A W2 will rarely have more than one or two connections in the town where she lives because her energy is an immediate turn-off. The associations the Wacko does have most likely tolerate the Wacko's behavior because they have to, as can be the case with coworkers and family members. We'll talk more about tolerating unavoidable Wackos in Chapter 17.

I know so much about W2 behavior because I forced myself to stomach the W2 wife of one of Ched's closest friends for ten years. I endured her antics because I didn't want to put a strain on Ched's friendship with her husband. I'll call this W2 "Debra." I am also pleased to now call her "history."

9 Characteristics of a
Wacko 2

W2s are fascinating specimens, capable of being completely charming one moment and completely psychotic the next. It's an in-between stage of Wackohood—sandwiched between the somewhat tolerable Wacko Level 1 and the higher echelons of Levels 3 and 4 where psychological intervention is desperately needed. And, like an awkward middle-schooler, a Level 2 Wacko has a highly unstable personality. In fact, the hallmark of Level 2 is the Jekyll and Hyde trait. W2s are people with whom you might carry on a perfectly pleasant conversation one minute, only to be on the receiving end of an abusive outburst the next. To make matters worse, the other qualities common among W2s only serve to fan the split-personality flames.

Keep in mind that W2s already embody some or all of the Wacko 1 traits, in addition to some or all of the following characteristics:

Who Am I Now? Dr. Jekyll or Mr. Hyde?
Watch Out for My "Look"
I'm Never Wrong—Ever!
The Best Offense is a Great Defense Mechanism
I'm Obsessive
I'm Paranoid

Dr. Jekyll and Mr. Hyde

The ease and speed with which W2s go from Dr. Jekyll to Mr. Hyde—that is, from sane to seriously demented—is absolutely astounding. The transformation is both rapid and unsettling, especially when witnessing it for the first time. An average conversation with a reasonably normal, rational person can suddenly turn into a low-budget horror flick when the Wacko unexpectedly bares his or her teeth and snarls over a seemingly insignificant disagreement. These alterations happen quickly and without warning. Then, just as swiftly, the light in the Wacko's eyes will flicker and the stable side of the Wacko's personality will return. A W2's paranoia and defensiveness keep her right on the edge at all times.

Level 2 Wackos are sort of fragile creatures when you think about it; they're so incapable of maintaining any consistent pattern of behavior. W2s are probably so exhausted from working on their "nice" act that it's almost a relief when they can unleash Mr. Hyde and give the good doctor a break.

I can think of no better example of a W2 than Debra, the wife of Ched's good friend, Keith. I don't know much about her family background, but I can surmise that she must have felt terribly out of control when she was young, because now she is one royal control freak, albeit one who is fashion challenged. Her wardrobe choices are as incongruous as her seemingly split personality, with loud patterns often layered atop dull brown solids. To an outsider, she would appear to be a typical, busy working woman. She knows how to smile and interact appropriately as long as events unfold precisely as she predicts. And therein lies the problem.

Dining with Debra was never uneventful. Once, when I was having an ordinary conversation with her during a luncheon, Mr. Hyde suddenly emerged without any provocation on my part. Debra started pointing a finger at me, saying, "Now you

wait a minute! What exactly do you mean by that comment?!"
Her teeth and gums were showing. When I first met Debra,
this type of behavior made me squirmy and uncomfortable.
But, by the time this particular occasion rolled around, I'd
experienced several hundred similar scenarios with her, so
I remained stoic. When I calmly clarified my comments, she
realized she was wrong and uttered, "Oh." Just that quickly
and effortlessly, Dr. Jekyll was back. W2s can't tolerate any
deviation from the carefully crafted scripts in their brains,
and Debra is no exception. The mere mention of a preference
for a different brand of toilet tissue can be enough to set her
off when the moment is right—or wrong, depending upon how
you look at it.

As we listened with the
interest of frozen peas, we
secretly kicked each other
under the table.

Speaking of dining experiences, a few years ago, Jessica came
to visit, and we went out for dinner and cocktails with Debra
and a group of other women. Jessica knew that I tolerated
Debra because of Ched, and the sympathy Jessica felt for me
was off the charts. Jessica could barely tolerate Debra as well.
Our dinner banter was polite and cordial and progressed
rather smoothly until somehow a child of mine became the
topic of our conversation. Debra kept going on and on about
how my child should be doing this and not doing that. W2s are
highly opinionated; trust me. As we listened with the interest

of frozen peas, Jessica and I secretly kicked each other under the table.

This would be a good time to elaborate on the "Jessica Method." Jessica developed this patronizing practice as a way to deal with the Wackos in her life. The Jessica Method is twofold: 1) use as few words as possible and 2) shut down the Wacko's conversations with carefully scripted comments. When a Wacko is playing expert, for example, calmly tilt your head to the side while saying, "Huh? Really? Wow!" You can build upon this method by making the face you give a three-year-old when he is telling you a long and in-depth story. You know, the "I'm interested in hearing everything you are saying" face. When you are tired of listening, a concise, clear comment to end the one-way conversation will shut up the Wacko, but be prepared for some fallout. "You might be right about that" is one of my favorite conversation-enders. Try it the next time you want a Wacko to clam up.

When Debra's lecture on my child-rearing habits seemed to be winding down, Jessica jumped at the chance to change the subject. Looking Debra square in the eyes, Jessica formed her calm, five-word response: "You shouldn't worry about it." Debra's attempt to force her opinions onto us had failed. Wackos hate to fail.

When Debra can't persuade her listeners, she loses it. When Debra can't persuade her listeners and she's been drinking, watch out! A second later, out jutted Debra's lower jaw, tense and teeth-baring. She said in a loud voice that shook the entire table, "Now wait a minute! I am around these children all the time and you don't even know them! Christina, did you hear what she just said to me?"

Meeting her gaze, I calmly answered her with one word: "Yes." I clearly felt she was out of line, and I had no intention of defending her irrational behavior. Silence enveloped our table as everyone stared at Debra.

It was an E. F. Hutton moment if there ever was one. She stared around the table, and we stared back. Then she got to her feet, adjusted the hairstyle she'd had for more than twenty years, looked over at Jessica, smiled and said, "It's so good to have you back in town. So where are you living now?" Everyone else went back to their own conversations as Jessica and I went back to kicking each other under the table. Mr. Hyde was put to rest for the time being. Using as few words as humanly possible really knocks Wackos off kilter.

The following story involving my neighbor is another great example of keeping things short 'n' sweet with a W2.

We had just moved into our new home—we had been there for about a week—when the doorbell rang for the first time. I put down the one-millionth box that I was unpacking and ran for the door. I was feeling keyed up about answering the new front door for the first time, and I was looking forward to meeting whoever was standing on the other side. I expected to see a smiling neighbor offering us a basket of homemade goodies or perhaps a plant. What I saw through the window of the front door, however, was not what I had expected.

There stood a neighbor with a look of complete contempt and disdain on his scowling face. I was thrown off balance for a minute, mentally trying to inventory our actions since we'd begun moving in. I couldn't think of anything we could have done to offend this person. My expression turned catatonic in reaction to his surly face. How dare he approach me this way? This was my home and my property. I braced myself, harnessed my personal power and prepared to have some sport with this guy to teach him a lesson.

I opened the door and smiled.

"Do you live here?" He asked in a low, angry tone through pursed lips.

I reached out my hand and shook his reluctant one, leaning way over as I did because he was quite short.

"Hi, I'm Christina. It's such a pleasure to meet you!" I gushed like a schoolgirl. The fun was just beginning.

He ignored my condescending tone and ranted, "Do you know there are children in this neighborhood?"

My eyes grew wide in fake shock as I calmly said while shaking my head from side to side, "I had no idea. I've only been here a few days and haven't seen any." If I was thinking faster on my feet I would have used a Southern accent just to add a little spice to the one-way conversation.

"Well," he continued, "your cars are going way too fast down the street and we could lose one of our kids!" Keep in mind that he's lecturing a caring, nurturing mother of three.

I looked at him square in the eye as I tilted my head and said, "Huh."

He was speechless for a second before he regained his footing and yelled some more. "There are about six kids who live on this street. My boys are afraid to go out into the street because of those cars!"

"Really?" I said as my eyes got bigger while continuing on with my act. I wasn't trying to be unsympathetic; I understand that a parent wouldn't appreciate someone driving too fast up and down a residential street. At this point, however, the question of speed was no longer the issue. The issue had become a clash of parental powers, and I was standing firm. I resented the way he verbally attacked me on my own property. If he were looking for an apology, he was going about it all the wrong way.

"If you could just let those cars know that they need to slow down that would solve the problem." He looked at me with scorn, while I wondered how I was supposed to have an intelligent conversation with my cars.

I responded with a huge, "Wow! I really appreciate your letting me know that. It was such a pleasure meeting you."

He was speechless and turned on his heels and left as angry as he was when he arrived.

This particular W2 showed up with all the looks a W2 owns, which you will read about next. He could have just as easily shown up, introduced himself nicely and stated his concerns. Although "those cars" did slow down, I chose not to take on his stuff.

When he left, I closed the door, shook my head and said outloud, "Welcome to the neighborhood, girlfriend."

The Look

The contorted facial expressions of a W2 in action deserve their own mention in the list of W2 character traits. Minus these carefully crafted and practiced "looks," a W2's countenance would be sorely lacking the dramatic punch that is so essential to a Wacko's psyche.

W2s have very specific faces for each situation that they perceive as a threat to their beliefs or brain power. Remember, for W2s it's their way or the highway, and believe me, they will wear their displeasure on their self-righteous sleeves. W2s will not hesitate to make faces at you when you talk about something new or different, if they want you to know they think you are an idiot or to express their anger. I call this trait "The Look." Watch for it, and if you see it you'll know you're dealing with at least a W2.

For the "I can't handle something new or different" look, expect a W2's eyes to shift to the side. The corner of her mouth will curl up on the same side. When you see this look, you can bet you are being tuned out.

If the Wacko thinks you are an idiot and wants the world to know it, expect her eyes to go straight to the ceiling during your conversation. This is her way of saying that she finds ceiling tiles more engaging than your comments. You can have some fun by looking up at the ceiling and asking her what's up there.

Somehow, her eyes will remain fixed and expressionless, and a full set of teeth and gums will be exposed.

The "I'm angry" look is rather disturbing. Somehow, her eyes will remain fixed and expressionless, and a full set of teeth and gums will be exposed. This is the scariest look of all because the Wacko will actually be smiling when she does this! I would consider this particular look, as well as the next two, to be warning signs that the Wacko is about to let loose with an outburst. Remember to duck if you happen to be dining so you aren't struck by any half-eaten food fragments.

Next would be the "I'm angry as hell look." Her pointer finger will come out, her bottom jaw will thrust forward, and only her bottom teeth and gums will be exposed as her eyes squint. It's a marvel of muscle control if you ask me. While Debra was certainly a master of all of the looks, she seemed particularly fond of this pointer finger method.

Last but not least is the "I know what you are saying or doing behind my back" look. Also known as the "I still act like I'm in elementary school" look. She'll squint while simultaneously puckering her mouth and sashaying her shoulders from side to side. Ick!

I'm Never Wrong Syndrome

Once again, we have a behavior pattern that warrants the label "syndrome" because it embodies the combination of several related traits. We learned from Level 1 Wackos that they can *do* no wrong, or at least they can't admit to it. W2s take this trait to a whole new height. The "I'm Never Wrong Syndrome" encompasses three traits: I'm Never Wrong, I Know it All and That's Not How it Happened at All. In other words, W2s can do no wrong, say no wrong and think no wrong.

Just remember that no matter what, W2s are always right and never wrong. If they get caught being wrong, they will never admit it and they certainly will never apologize. W2s have thick playbooks full of defensive maneuvers, and the "I'm Never Wrong Syndrome" is one of their favorites.

To illustrate how this syndrome affects others, I'll relay a story to you about Debra and Keith's trip to Europe. When Ched and I had dinner with them upon their return, Keith told a story about Debra at the wheel of the rental car in Europe. They were on a narrow stretch of road, and Debra was having trouble managing the twists and turns. "I asked her to let me take the wheel, because she seemed to be having trouble," Keith told us, "But she insisted that she was doing just fine."

Keith then added with nervous laughter that he was afraid they were going to crash. He tried to make light of her driving in his retelling of the story, but I could sense that he had felt truly afraid at the time.

"Why didn't you insist that she pull over?" I asked Keith when Debra was away from the table.

"Are you kidding?" he asked. "Telling her what to do would have made things worse than a car crash!" I can just picture Debra in the driver's seat, looking like Miss Gulch from *The Wizard of OZ*, pedaling hysterically down the lane to get Dorothy's dog with her chin jutting forward and an upside-down smile.

Another example would be when Keith and Debra sought counseling for marital problems. It was a complete waste of time and money. Debra's "I'm Never Wrong Syndrome" rendered her incapable of shouldering any of the blame. Debra was content as long as her husband's digressions were the topic of conversation, but once the therapist started pointing questions in her direction, things changed dramatically. "Now wait a minute!" She sternly corrected the therapist. "I see where this is going, and I have nothing to say about my childhood. My childhood was great. This is about him, not me!" Well, that was the end of their counseling to improve their marriage.

W2s truly believe they know everything. Combine the "I'm never wrong" factor with the "I know it all" factor, and what do you get? A certifiable pain in the ass, that's what.

I decided to introduce Debra to my pal Danielle over cocktails. Petite and pale-skinned with long, black hair, Danielle had a fragile air about her. But looks can be deceiving.

We arrived at the bar for drinks and started chatting. Sitting across from Danielle was Debra, whose brown outfit was topped with a multicolored jacket that was lousy with shiny gold buttons. Danielle mentioned that she'd like to fly her mother in from Canada, but she couldn't find a reasonably priced ticket.

"Oh, that's not true. You can get online and find a good one," Debra cut in.

"I already tried that, and nothing is available for the dates I need," Danielle said politely.

This conversation might sound innocent enough to the uninitiated, but I could see the storm brewing.

"That's not true," Debra kept saying. I knew that she wanted the last word and that she would lower her head and plow straight through Danielle in her pursuit to be right.

Petite and pale-skinned with long, black hair, Danielle had a fragile air about her. But looks can be deceiving.

What Debra didn't know about Danielle is that she is savvy, and she is thorough. When she says she can't find a reasonable ticket and she has tried everything, trust me, she has. At this point, I started guzzling the rum and Diet Coke in my hand as I watched the human know-it-all freight train barreling down the track. This conversation went on for about ten more minutes as Danielle tried in vain to fight her off. In the meantime, I beckoned for another rum and Coke and braced myself for the collision to come.

Then, the moment I had been waiting for arrived in all its glory. Danielle tilted her head to the side, looked Debra right in the eyes and uttered these five words: "You know what? Bite me!"

Debra was set back for a second. She tugged her brown hair away from her freckled face, then shot back with, "Excuse me? That's rude!"

Danielle put her head down and fell silent. I guzzled some more of my cocktail while trying to numb myself. This was not the Danielle I knew. She'd lost her spunk Then Danielle looked up and lowered her eyelids. "Allow me to rephrase that statement," she said with an icy calm. "Fucking bite me!" She didn't let me down after all. She calls it her French Canadian temper. I call it standing up for herself. Ah-bdee, ah-bdee, ah-bdee, that's all folks!

Mr. Hyde scurried away immediately. Debra behaved herself for the rest of the night but made jokes about Danielle the next day, convinced she was right and that Danielle was unbalanced.

Don't waste your breath trying to explain to a W2 how others perceive his or her behavior. When I tried to play peace-keeper and explain to Debra why Danielle wasn't exactly taken with her, all I got was a self-righteous finger in my face and an adamant, "That's not how it happened at all!" Wackos remember things the way they want to remember them. Most Wacko brains automatically generate new versions of any memories that were originally unpleasant, especially if the Wacko was wrong.

For example, I once made the mistake of casually discussing the political situation in Russia with Debra. I told her that my friend Ilsa said that it is still difficult to get out of Russia and that if you leave and return you can be treated cruelly.

"That's not true! Russia is no longer communist," she spat at me, displaying her "I think you are an idiot" look.

I calmly explained that Ilsa wouldn't lie and that, in fact, she receives email from her friends in Russia asking for advice on how to get out. I should have saved my breath. I was dispensing way too much information and using way too many words. My explanation merely fueled Debra's fire, and she became relentless; she had to be right. She continued to disagree with me while staring straight ahead at the television. She lacked even the common courtesy to look in my direction as we argued. After realizing my initial mistake, I calmly asked her, using four words only, "Why would Ilsa lie?"

That question was the trigger. Debra smiled her ghoulish grimace with her teeth and gums exposed and said sarcastically, "I don't know why she would tell you these lies!"

She had me right where she wanted me. She wanted me to get angry and I did.

"Do you realize that you always have to be right?" I snapped at her while keeping my gaze fixed on the TV.

It was Debra who looked away from the TV first. Or should I say, Mr. Hyde. She looked at me with her bottom jaw tensed and her gums exposed and responded quickly with, "Do you realize you don't know what you are talking about?"

What was I to say? It was like arguing with a third-grader. I just sat there as Debra gradually morphed back into Dr. Jekyll and continued to watch television as if the entire conversation had never happened.

After that encounter I began to realize I wanted this person out of my life simply because she was giving me the willies. I knew there was no point in trying to convince her that she was misinformed because she knows everything anyway.

Several months later when Debra met Ilsa, Debra asked about the situation in Russia. Ilsa shared the exact information that I had shared with Debra.

"This is what I tried telling you, but you wouldn't listen," I said to Debra, feeling like I was going to explode from all my suppressed frustration.

"That's not how it happened at all!" Debra wailed.

The Best Offense is a Great Defense Mechanism

W2s have so many defense mechanisms, it's a wonder they don't drive themselves right out of existence. Three of the most effective strategies in their mental playbook of defensive maneuvers include being judgmental, selfish and nosey.

W2s judge others to mask their own insecurities. It's the oldest trick in the book—criticize someone else's way of living, for example, before anyone realizes who the inferior one truly is.

Debra would flex her judgmental muscles by refusing to call me Christina.

"Why do you call yourself Christina? That isn't your name," she would say.

My response was always the same: "Ched started calling me Christina and I love it. In fact, I would prefer it if you would call me Christina instead of Christine."

It didn't matter how many times I explained my preferences to Debra. Her skull was way too thick.

"Well, that isn't your name, so I'm not going to call you that."

I felt like I was talking to a five-year-old. That was three years ago, and Debra called me Christine every chance she had until I dumped her. You'll hear more about that soon.

W2s are also exceedingly selfish. They call this play whenever they need a personal power boost.

Ched and I had four friends from out of town staying at our home. All together there were nine of us. One evening, I was dim-witted enough to invite Debra and Keith to join our group for dinner. When the meal was over, I asked them to return for breakfast in the morning, as I made a big deal about making omelets with the leftovers. At 8:30 a.m., our guests started waking up. We tried to postpone breakfast until we heard from Debra and Keith, but we were getting too hungry to wait. We finally heard from Debra at 10:30. I told her that we had started eating but to come on over and join in the fun.

"We are on our way right now," Debra said.

All nine of us waited another hour and a half for the two of them to show up. We were living in a lovely resort town at the time and we were all eager to get out of the house and go do something fun. When they finally walked in the door at noon I politely asked Debra where they were. "When we heard you were eating leftovers we went out," Keith answered. All nine of us were speechless. I said nothing as I tried to create a conflict-free environment with this self-absorbed couple. I said, "I'm sorry about the mix-up, but you guys said you were coming for breakfast."

"I find it quite interesting that you are apologizing one moment and blaming us the next," Keith told me with a full set of teeth and gums showing as he smiled.

Oh my God, I thought, *he's been Wackoized!*

Debra was clearly behind the whole debacle. She stood there smugly not saying a word.

Her control over Keith always confounded me. He's a successful corporate man with several college degrees and most certainly should be able to think for himself. None of us understand the dynamics of their relationship.

W2s also gain power by gaining information. They don't feel guilty about delving into your personal paperwork because they can't help themselves. It's the old "I'd rather examine their stuff than my own" routine. Don't leave any bills, letters or confidential documents lying around if you have a W2 in your life. Even if you're being cautious with printed information, Wackos can find ways for you to inadvertently spill your own beans during a seemingly innocent conversation. You might hear something like, "You know, I ran into a friend the other day who just bought a new laptop." I got caught in this trap myself once and said, "Yeah, me too!" I should have spotted the red flag immediately when she said she "ran into a friend." She doesn't have any friends.

Wacko 2s also gain power by gaining information.

W2s are experts at getting information out of people and will often try to make those around them feel guilty for not 'fessing up sooner—as if they are entitled to everyone's personal scoop. A Wacko's obsessive personality fuels her desire for dirty laundry. And she is almost never satisfied. One tiny tidbit of information will only make her hunger for more. On the other hand, if you ask a W2 for personal information, expect the Wacko's eyes to narrow and her mouth to pucker. The W2's paranoia will take over and she'll start needling you to find out why you're so interested. Knowing your personal information makes a W2 feel in control. Dispensing her own private details makes her feel vulnerable.

Obsessive? Me?

Obsessive behavior comes with the W2 territory. When a Wacko gets his mind fixated on something, he will obsess for hours, months or years, depending upon the situation. If a Wacko is angry with someone because she feels she has been treated unjustly, her paranoia will blend with her obsession to create a deadly emotional nuclear bomb prone to detonating without warning.

Once, a W2 I knew very briefly hired a personal trainer to help her become certified in Pilates. Brenda's training with the instructor was intense; they worked together several times a week. I stood on the sidelines and waited for the day when the instructor couldn't deal with Brenda one more moment. I knew that her rude, self-righteous behavior and annoying "looks" would rapidly wear thin. As I suspected, the instructor severed the relationship after about a month. Frankly, I was surprised that anyone could have spent that much time with a full-fledged W2.

First came Brenda's shock and embarrassment; next came her anger and obsession. "Why does this always happen to me?" she whined to me over the phone.

I couldn't believe it came out of my mouth, but I actually said, "Well, maybe she just doesn't like you. It's not the end of the world." I thought I had gotten through to her.

But, true to W2 form, Brenda obsessed for days on end until she had convinced herself that it was entirely the instructor's fault. Once she was back on her Wacko feet, she put her attack plan in motion. She made phone calls and she mailed letters telling the instructor she was rude and unprofessional. When she told me that she would sue for libel if she found out the trainer *said* anything bad about her, I gently corrected her that libel is the written word.

"You mean defamation of character or slander, right?" I asked her.

She shook her head with her "You idiot" look and said, "No, I mean libel!"

Brenda just wouldn't accept reality and move on. Two weeks later I had the distinct displeasure of witnessing one of Brenda's tirades. She repeatedly gripped and ungripped her hands, her jaw locked, her neck muscles flexing. "I'm so angry that I just want to take it out on someone!" she fumed. Well, that someone was me. I said I knew her "very briefly" and that's why.

Who Me? Paranoid

W2s are perpetually paranoid that people are doing or saying things about them behind their backs. Expect this behavior as long as they are alive or perhaps until they've entered into therapy, which is highly improbable.

A few years ago, Ched and I made plans with our good friends for both our families to go away together over the holidays. We made the reservations a year in advance, and I was so looking forward to vacationing with our best friends. I purposely said nothing about the trip to Debra and Keith because there were two things I was certain of: 1) She would definitely want to come along; and 2) She would ruin the trip. Then one night about three weeks before the trip, while we were having cocktails, Ched accidentally spilled our plans to Keith, and Debra overheard. My lungs completely deflated. I wanted to stomp my feet like an angry child. We had kept it a secret for so long.

I could tell from Debra's expression that she was unnerved that we would make these secret plans. In her paranoid, self-centered little mind, she was probably envisioning the rest of us spending our vacation gabbing about her behind her back. In this case, she was right about one thing: I did do something behind her back, and I was committed to getting away with it! Debra unraveled before our eyes, and her look turned acidic. She was seething.

She was right about one thing: I did do something behind her back, and I was committed to getting away with it!

I instantly lapsed into Mother Teresa mode and tried my hardest to curtail the fallout.

"Last year when we made the same plans, you said you had no interest in driving a few hours away and bringing all the food," I explained kindly. "You said that you prefer to spend the holidays at home." All the while a tiny voice inside my head was warning me, *Too many words, Christina. Too. Many. Words.*

Out sprang the angry eyes and full set of teeth and gums through an obviously forced smile. She looked straight ahead—not in my eyes—and barked, "That was last year."

Being The Pleaser, I expressed remorse and said that if I had known she felt that way, we would have rented a bigger place. All I needed to do was keep my mouth shut and let it drop. But I failed to realize silence was my strongest ally in this situation.

Anyway, Debra cooled her jets and said, "Oh don't worry. We will find a place of our own. I'll call immediately on Monday." It had to be her paranoia, and not hurt feelings, that made her willing to drop everything and make last-minute plans to leave for the holidays.

You can imagine my euphoria when she called Monday and said she couldn't find a place. You can also imagine my devastation when she called an hour later to say she found a place. I suspected that the first phone call was just a sick joke. I was screwed. Really screwed.

From the moment Debra and Keith arrived, the entire energy inside the rented house shifted from pleasurable to pure anxiety. Everyone walked on eggshells, waiting for her next tirade, negative comment or judgment. Ilsa got the ball rolling.

On the first full day of our stay in the rented house, Ilsa walked through the kitchen wearing a beautiful shirt that I bought for myself but never wore. I gave it to Ilsa as a gift with my undying devotion and affection. When Debra saw the shirt her eyes narrowed and her lips formed a prissy, airtight scowl. "Isn't that your shirt that your friend has on," Debra asked me after Ilsa had left the room. Debra was fuming. I considered saying, "Why the look? Why would that bother you?" But instead, I said nothing. I was beginning to learn from my past mistakes.

I casually left the kitchen to get away from Debra. Later, Debra spotted me talking to Ilsa about our plans for the day. Out of earshot, Debra must have assumed that she was the topic of our conversation.

When I ran into Debra later on, she looked me square in the eyes and shook her head from side to side with her mouth hanging open in a slight smile. "Well, well, well. Were you and your friend having a nice conversation about me?" Her tight lips puckered up and her shoulders swayed first one way and then the other.

Her body language was so eight-year-old I wanted to vomit. Damn it! She was ruining my trip! I did what I had done for more than ten years; I said nothing and put up with her antics. I went on with my afternoon, keeping everything inside and not discussing my frustration or disappointment with anyone. I didn't want to give Debra the satisfaction of knowing what an awful time I was having because of her.

By the end of the trip I had been smacked by the two-by-four. I was done. I allowed her to ruin something I had been looking forward to all year. Once we were home, I told Ched I was done with Debra and that I hoped it wouldn't affect his friendship with Keith.

Debra called me a few weeks after the trip. I got to the point and curtly informed her that I didn't want to have anything more to do with her. She asked me why, but when I tried to answer her she interrupted me constantly to defend her behavior. Realizing that my attempt at an explanation was a wasteless use of oxygen, I reverted to the five-word method.

When she started ranting and raving my response was, "This is what I mean."

Finally, she ran out of defenses. "So, what you are trying to say is that you don't want to have anything to do with me anymore, right?"

"Yes, that's correct," I answered. Three words—nicely done! It was finally over.

Or so I thought.

Chapter 10

Lessons Learned

There are two lessons I'd like you to learn from my discussions about W2 behavior.

The first is to never enter into a relationship with a W2 just to appease your spouse, friend, mother, etc. Let the two parties who are actually friends co-mingle while you steer clear of the Wacko. Being cordial in unavoidable social situations and chance encounters is one thing; attempting to socialize on your own time with a W2 is another. I tried it for Ched's sake, but it wasn't necessary. Learn from me and don't waste more than ten years going out of your way to tolerate a W2. Speak your truth to this type and watch them go away quickly. If you keep your mouth shut and put up with their deplorable behavior, that is all you will be doing—indefinitely.

Lesson Two is to keep the dialogue short and sweet when defending your opinions and actions. State your place clearly and concisely—in five words or fewer if possible—and move on to another topic. You will never change a W2's mind, so don't waste your energy.

Remember that holiday vacation that Debra and Keith decided to crash? A few months after the trip, I received a letter from Debra. You'll have to read it to believe it.

> Dear Christine,
>
> I am sorry for any behavior that **you** feel was inappropriate during the trip. I've given things a great amount of thought and I have come to the conclusion that the two of us are very different. You are into things and do things very differently than myself. Perhaps you feel threatened by me? I'm moving on with my life.
>
> Sincerely,
> Debra

Here was my response:

> Dear Debra,
>
> First of all, I would like to thank you for all of the generosity you have shown my family and me over the years. However, my decision to end our friendship has nothing to do with the two of us being different. I love that about all of my friends.
> The reason I can't engage in this relationship is simply because I can't deal with your anger anymore, and the children feel the same way as well. Your anger is particularly worse when you drink.
> I am glad that you are moving on with your life and wish you nothing but the best.
>
> Sincerely,
> Christina

About two weeks later, I received another letter with the name **Christine Eckert** on the front. Ched and I looked at how the letter was addressed, and I sent it back. My response to her second letter consisted of exactly zero words, and I have never heard from her again.

The hallmark trait of a W2 is the rapid transformation between Jekyll and Hyde. W2s also make their feelings painfully clear with a "look" like no other when they feel threatened. And they feel threatened quite often, because they are perpetually paranoid and they can never allow themselves to be wrong. They obsess endlessly about meaningless issues and their list of defensive plays is one hundred yards long.

You will find interacting in a consistent, stable manner rather difficult, if not impossible, with Wackos of this level. Socialize sparingly if you must mingle at all.

Where the Scary Things Are

Y ou have my absolute permission to judge this book by its cover. I didn't call this book *Do You Have Wackos in Your Life?* I titled it *Winning Against the Wackos in Your Life* because I am so confident that every person out there has had a run-in with a Wacko, whether you recognized it as Wacko behavior at the time or not. I am so certain of this, that my book's title assumes it.

I have had the distinct displeasure of being involved with each and every unsavory level of Wacko—primarily due to my host personality. For most Wackos, the pinnacle of Wackohood is Wacko Level 3—where the scary stuff starts happening. And, it was my experiences with a Wacko 3 (W3) that compelled me to write this book. Fortunately, I am about to arm you with the knowledge you need to recognize and, therefore, avoid this type, so that you don't repeat my mistakes. Spotting a W3 is simple if you just watch, look and listen.

Watch for the "help me" look, which a W3 will often use to lure his or her prey. But don't be fooled. She wants you to think of her as the victim, but trust me when I say that it's the other way around. You'll depart the relationship feeling like you've been flattened by a steamroller. *Look* for a constant state of chaos surrounding the Wacko, and *listen* for non-stop, one-way conversations in which the topic is always the Wacko herself. I'm convinced that W3s deal with their psychological dysfunctions by making sure they are the center of attention at all costs. *At all costs.*

Wacko 3s Don't Have Friends

We learned previously that any circle of friends will shrink dramatically as a Wacko's behavior progresses to Level 2. Most Wackos, Level 3s included, are desperate to feel accepted and loved. Unfortunately, they don't know how to love and accept others. A W2's paranoia and defense mechanisms will typically start to wear thin on those around her, but a W3 will actually take calculated steps to drive away anyone who moves in too close. My best guess as to why they do this is because they were "dumped" so many times in the past that drawing first blood is now the only way they can feel empowered. W3s are so confident that every relationship will eventually end in disaster that they actually seek to choreograph and control the speed and circumstances of the collapse to give them a false sense of supremacy.

The Seven Steps of Relationship Demolition

When it comes to a W3 engaging in a healthy, loving relationship, let's just say she's like a house that has been on the market for too long. As my real estate agent said, "If it doesn't sell right away, there's something wrong with it." That's why, more often than not, a W3 is alone, or she will be eventually.

A W3 will ultimately drive a wedge between herself and anyone who gets within close proximity. Living with the status quo provides no drama, so she must manufacture some. A W3 will cause the demise of her relationships by employing the following seven steps:

STEP ONE: The first step is the baited hook—the way in which a Wacko draws in an unsuspecting "friend." A W3 will act engaging and initially interested in a lover or friend and supportive of his or her needs, and periodically throughout the relationship as the need suits. She may occasionally do extreme favors for the innocent would-be victim or offer gifts that seem disproportionately lavish. Many people fall for this over-the-top outpouring of kindness. Don't mistake larger-than-life generosity for true friendship. She's overcompensating to keep you engaged.

STEP TWO: After a brief period of time, a W3 will start talking for hours, days, weeks and months about the people in her life who have wronged her. She will insult and talk behind the backs of people she holds near and dear as "friends." If she is talking trash about others, why would you think you would be an exception?

It's been awhile since we've repeated our mantra, so let's say it together now: *How it begins is how it ends.*

A W3 can go on for hours talking about her boss, the boss's wife, the boss's kids and how dysfunctional they all are. If you think she isn't going to talk trash about you behind your back, you're deluding yourself. A W3 brings down everyone in her life to build herself up and take center stage. I once confronted a W3 about her constant backstabbing. Her response was disturbing. "You see, Christina, everyone talks about each other behind their backs. We all do it," she sneered. I wanted to respond with, "Speak for yourself, honey," but I didn't want to waste any more of my breath. With her distorted view of reality, I'm sure she believed that what she was saying was true.

Please watch, look and listen for Step Two of this process. This is one of the easiest signs of a W3 to recognize. When you see it, take a permanent "vay-cay" from this person.

STEP THREE: As Step Three unfolds, the Wacko will begin to blatantly belittle and molest your self-esteem by igniting petty arguments and being overly confrontational. She will try to provoke you by pointing out all of your imperfections—whether they're real or figments of her unbalanced mind. This step marks the beginning of the end. She has decided that you are no longer serving any purpose other than to help her create a new drama that she can bitch about later to her next unsuspecting victims.

STEP FOUR: This is the "dirty laundry" step. Everything you say can and will be used against you. Prepare to have any of your past actions or inactions thrown into your face. I've previously advised you to never share private information with a Wacko. This is especially important if you're dealing with a W3. Believe me when I say that the Wacko will make note of every detail, and these details will resurface during Step Four. Never let a W3 engage you in a conversation that compels you to share personal information. A duck may look like it is bobbing passively on a tranquil lake, but what those webbed feet are doing beneath the surface is a different story.

If you ever stick around long enough to reach Step Four, you should also be prepared to be compared with the actions and characteristics of every past friend or lover. Nothing you do will ever be as grand as the actions of those who have gone before you. The Wacko will use these comparisons as well as old grudges to create conflict with her newest "friend."

My last W3 was actually trying to alienate her own sister, so she used our "friendship" as a shining example. During one of her self-involved marathon phone conversations, the Wacko told me that she told her younger sister I was a better friend to her than her sister was. I told her I was uncomfortable about that and felt she was lucky to have a sister who loved her so much. My sentiments soared right over her head, and she proceeded to cause dissention within her family, which had supported her unconditionally for more than thirty years.

STEP FIVE: The end is near when a Wacko reaches Step Five. A Wacko uses this step to begin physically removing herself from the drama she has created. She will conveniently leave the scene so that those left behind must pick up the pieces.

STEP SIX: Departing from a relationship with a Wacko is never easy, especially with a W3. After she has made her well-rehearsed dramatic exit, she will try to destroy the victim left behind. She will write emails, make phone calls, do drive-bys if she lives close enough, threaten the victim with a restraining order and call her other "friends" to share the drama while it's fresh in her mind, all while painting the most unflattering picture of the victim. This is the Wacko's way of squeezing out every last drop of drama, and it provides her with a quick fix of her favorite drug: pandemonium.

STEP SEVEN: This is the "recycling step" in which the Wacko will use your former relationship with her as the ice-breaker in her new relationships. You will now become the "victimizer" she talks about to lure unsuspecting spectators in closer. If she finds a willing listener, the vicious cycle will start again.

12 Characteristics of a
Wacko 3

If I'm remembering the second law of thermodynamics correctly, things naturally go from order to disorder—to interpret it broadly. Wackos are no exception. Their personalities will go from bad to worse as their desire for greater and greater control triggers new Wacko traits. A W1 will develop into a W2 if the W1 traits are no longer serving a purpose. Some Wackos will idle at Level 1 or 2 indefinitely; some, in pursuit of bigger power trips, will forge ahead into the darkest reaches of Level 3, where things start turning grisly.

A W3's world is primarily chaotic, and every conversation with her is littered with non-stop complaints. In fact, the hallmark of Level 3 is constant chaos. No aspect of a W3's life is stable for very long.

The following W3 traits serve to perpetuate the mayhem in her life and help her complete the seven steps of destruction we just talked about:

Pandemonium is My Drug
I Live on the Phone
I Am Self-Absorbed
I Am Emotionally Unstable
I Hold Grudges

Pandemonium is My Drug

W3s simply cannot function unless their life is chaotic. A Wacko of this level will continuously chisel away at any semblance of normalcy present in his or her life until it degrades into disorder. She will never be satisfied with her marriage—no matter how fulfilling it appears to be; she will never get along well with her in-laws; she will never be content with her job; she will never be happy with her friends or the way she looks or the way her house looks. You name it, a W3 hates it. Nothing in this person's life will ever be good enough. If it were, she would have less for which to complain.

A W3's drug is pandemonium, administered 'round the clock. And she gives new meaning to the label Drama Queen. She can turn any molehill into Mt. Everest. She's the type who seems to *create* problems. She feeds off turmoil. And she will drag any willing listener into her science fiction reality.

A Wacko 3's drug is pandemonium, administered 'round the clock.

Most women would avoid hosting a baby shower for a friend the same weekend as her own child's first birthday party, for example. But that's exactly why she undertakes such a huge responsibility—because most women wouldn't dream of attempting it. She wants people talking about her and making comparisons. She wants everyone thinking that she is attempting the impossible. She wants the world to see her as a survivor of insurmountable odds. She wants people to think, *Poor thing; I can't believe everything she has to do to make this weekend successful.* She will energetically fuel these conversations by half-bragging/half-complaining about the all-nighter she has to pull so she can take down the birthday decorations, clean the house and redecorate for the shower. She will portray herself as a victim of unavoidable poor timing, even though she created this situation herself. She wants her own personal pandemonium to be on the minds of everyone around her. The more complicated her life is, the happier she is. She will complain about the baby shower to everyone who will listen, with the exception of the very pregnant guest of honor.

W3s emit this energy that says "I'm a victim. Why does this always happen to me?" Don't fall for it. It's those around the Wacko who are being victimized, trust me. If you've ever tried to maintain a relationship with this type of person, you know how exhausting it can be to be caught in the Wacko's whirlwind of chaos and complaints. A W3 can't live without constant commotion. But you can.

I Live On the Phone

W3s cannot survive without chaos, and they cannot survive if no one else knows about it. That's why W3s live on the phone when they are not in the physical company of another human being. A W3 has to constantly be sharing her drama morning, noon and night. After all, what good is a play if no one is watching? When she is not at home on the phone, a W3 is on her cell phone talking about herself. A W3 feels compelled to blab incessantly about her most recent tragedy and the person who has taken advantage of her, used her, abused her, offended her, upended her, etc. It's like some freakish cable network carrying the all-complaints channel: all complaints, all day, all night. You're hearing just one side of each story, of course, and it will make you wonder if the complaints would even exist if there was no one to listen to them. It's the old tree falling in the forest question. Would she really have anything to whine about if she didn't have a captive cochlear audience?

Keep in mind if you happen to be caught on the phone with a W3 that she is not looking for advice or feedback. Don't even open your mouth. If you try to offer some words of wisdom, a W3 will talk at the same exact time you are, not listening to a word you are saying. She will not pause; she will not miss a beat. When you stop talking, she'll keep on going, completely unaware that you were trying to interject some enlightenment upon the subject.

I Am Self-Absorbed

W3s are not a little self-absorbed; they are not a lot self-absorbed; they are self-absorbed at the cellular level.

W3s are so completely into themselves that they don't even realize that they are friendless. When you first meet a W3, her deep level of self-absorption might not be readily discernible. She is restraining herself because she is baiting the hook. This usually doesn't last long. If she senses that you are a willing listener, she'll open the gates and you'll find yourself flooded of information. Don't mistake this outpouring of personal details as a sign of trust and true friendship. This is where most innocent people falter. Wackos can be smooth. They can be charming. They can play the part of victim with Oscar-worthy ease. Then, when your heart is open and you are naive enough to believe you have made a new friend, the hurricane blows in. Your so-called relationship will go from a pretend mutual admiration society to a very real self-admiration society.

If you embody the Mother Teresa Syndrome, make yourself comfortable on the sofa when the phone rings because you'll be listening to the Wacko talk about herself for hours, months and years. Every time a W3 I knew called me, the conversation would start out with what amounted to a rhetorical greeting: "Hi, Christina! How are you?"

I would reply, "I'm fine, how are you?"

And off she'd go.

As you can imagine, this would go on for hours as I would listen to her talk about herself and how victimized she had been since the last time we talked. Whenever I couldn't handle one more minute of her hollow solicitations for advice, I would graciously excuse myself to drop off my toddler at pre-school and hang up. Never mind that sometimes it was a Saturday. She never noticed—why would she? I never felt guilty because I knew she was on the phone talking someone else's ear off within seconds.

When a W3 is in full-blown blabbing mode, he or she will ignore anything and everything going on around her. I once had a W3 in my life who would cry uncontrollably on the phone to me while bellowing, "I hate everyone! I'm suicidal! I hate my child!" She would say these things with her child right there in the room with her. No one else existed but her, and it showed. I am deeply ashamed for not telling her to shut her pie hole and grow up.

Just assume that anytime a W3 asks you how you are, she really doesn't want to know. If you try to talk about yourself and the things going on in your life, don't expect a captive audience. Trust me when I say that she is waiting for you to pause so that she can change the subject back to all things Wacko. I'm convinced that the inventor of Caller ID had a W3 in his or her life. One time, as a joke, I put my phone down for six minutes and left the room. When I returned, I picked the phone up and W3 was still talking about herself.

One time, as a joke, I put my phone down for six minutes and left the room. When I returned she was still talking about herself.

Maureen, a W3, was my inspiration for writing this book, so no description of W3 behavior would be complete without stories about her.

Maureen epitomized self-absorption. She and I once met her sister and brother-in-law, who is a successful entrepreneur, for dinner. Maureen actually had the audacity to be confrontational with Jared and argue with his business acumen. I don't think he was able to get two sentences out without being interrupted.

The sister looked over at me at one point and said, "She's stubborn."

If I had felt about her then the way I do now, my reply would have been, "She's not stubborn; she's just mentally unhinged."

Maureen never even acknowledged that I was sitting at the same table. Everything she said revolved around "My company, my company, my company." Finally I had to interrupt their conversation and say firmly, "*Our* company."

Later on in the one-way conversation, I proudly mentioned an idea that I'd developed. At that moment, Jared turned to me with narrowed eyes and said, "You mean *both* of your ideas." He had been Wackoized! I knew at that moment that she had kept this poor newlywed on the phone for hours on end complaining about me. W3s only want others to hear their side of every story, so that the Wackos can always be right. I'm wondering when Jared would catch on and start checking his Caller ID.

If you think that you can outsmart a Wacko by writing her an email message to make your point, think again. I tried that with Maureen. She still didn't "listen" to my written words. In fact, she complained that I was taking up too much of her time discussing my friends, my problems, my children, etc. Well, shiver me timbers! For the first and only time since I had met her, I was impressed. She actually knew the names of all my children.

I also tried unsuccessfully to sever our business relationship via email. I told her that "I could in no way be in a business relationship with someone as emotionally unbalanced as you are." All this did was put words in her mouth. I eventually had to contact a lawyer to help me get out of the business mess I'd helped create through my passivity. I later found out that Maureen told *my* lawyer, "You know, Christina is really *unbalanced*." She gave my attorney the chills.

A W3 loves to take her own personal insanity and dump it in your lap while pointing an accusing finger at you.

I Am Emotionally Uncontrollable

A W3 is pretty much "un" everything: *un*stable, *un*controllable, *un*hinged, *un*balanced, *un*sound, *un*manageable—you name it. What is so mind-boggling is that W3s are completely *un*aware of their emotional disturbances.

A dead giveaway that you're dealing with a W3 is if she changes her mind incessantly. What's disconcerting to people like me is a W3's ability to constantly change her story and pretend that prior conversations never took place. You never want to be a bridesmaid if the bride and maid of honor are W3s. They'll change the dress color and shoe style at least a dozen times—after you've paid for the stuff.

Good luck trying to keep your feet on the ground when a W3 is whipping you around in her emotional air stream. W3s certainly don't listen to other people, and apparently, they don't listen to themselves, either.

Several years ago, a W3 I knew called me one night to ask why her child was not being invited to slumber parties. I politely lied and said that I couldn't possibly know the answer to her question. She reassured me in a calm voice, "I need to know so I can help her."

This disarmed me enough to answer her as honestly as I could. "Well, I've heard your daughter has been spreading lies about the other girls, and she apparently has a habit of repeating confidences that were entrusted to her."

Within seconds, she came *un*glued. "That is not true! My child is sweet and would never do that! I watch how she interacts with other children, and she is very respectful. I'm pulling her out of school!" I don't know what child she "watched." It was always my impression that she watched nothing—she was always on the phone.

While I can understand a mother wanting to defend her daughter, I wasn't braced for the vehemence. I continued to speak calmly with her despite her *un*reasonable state of mind. My efforts, surprisingly, were not in vain. I finally got through to her—after about four hours, but what the heck. Can I get a Brownie Badge, please? All kids can do schmucky things in school—including my own. Children were born to embarrass us and humble us; those of us with level heads understand this. W3s handle things differently from other people. They will soar to the outer limits of deranged, ridiculous behavior when their imperfections are exposed. Apparently, they will soar to these same outer limits even when their children's imperfections are exposed.

Being a host, I apologized for answering her question. "I wish I hadn't said anything," I told her while suffering the effects from her torrential outpouring of psychosis through the phone.

After her exhausting tirade, W3 said, "You're not my best friend anymore."

You can imagine my bewilderment after hearing such a juvenile announcement. Being the host that I am, I didn't want to upset her even more by telling her how infantile I found her behavior. Truthfully, I was relieved to have found a way out in, as my daughter's friend Kaitlan would say, a "ginormous" way.

It was at this point that I said to myself, Where is the two-by-four? I'll hit myself on the head with it!

As the "law of ridiculous coincidences" would have it, I ran into this W3 the next morning. She looked exhausted and raw, like she'd been up all night trying to justify her child's behavior to herself. It was at this point that I said to myself, *Where is the two-by-four? I'll hit myself on the head with it!* A W3 loves to make Andes out of anthills.

I Hold a Grudge

Like an elephant, W3s remember everything; however, they will only admit to remembering the things you did that they didn't like. When your relationship starts getting stormy, you'll discover just how deep a W3's memory runs. Being masters of grudge-holding, a W3 can regurgitate copious details of disturbing events—from the crib to the current date. As you already know, because of the W3's inadequate listening skills, she won't remember that you apologized, either. Apologies are conveniently forgotten. Her irrepressibly compulsive behavior will in no doubt lead her to persistently bring up things you have done that she didn't like. (Which, by the way, is pretty much everything.) You can repeat your apologies all you want, but it won't stop her. W3s are like horses wearing blinders, and the only things that matter are the power-trip payoffs dangling in front of them. You aren't the only one who will have to listen to the Wacko unloading all of the unflattering instances about you that she has mentally cataloged. Everyone else in her life will suffer the misery of having their ears talked off about the Wacko's issues with you.

The most amusing part of watching a W3 come unglued is when she releases all of her stored-up grudges at once. When a W3 is ready for war, she will practically foam at the mouth while repeating for the one-millionth time everything you have done in the past that upset her. Don't even try to interrupt her or stop her. This unbridled release of pent-up grudges is a natural component of Step Four—when you have reached the pinnacle of your relationship and everything is about to crumble. I like to call it Close Encounters of the Third Wacko Level Kind.

Here's another Maureen story to illustrate the point.

Seven months into my business partnership with Maureen, things started rapidly deteriorating, and she stunned me with the announcement that she had never liked the web site that my son created for our business. Keep in mind that throughout the process, I had repeatedly asked Maureen for her approval of the site. "It's fine," she *always* said. But, when it suited her, she changed her story and used the web site as just another bone to gnaw on and tear to shreds.

When I asked her why she didn't say something sooner about the web site, the "businesswoman's" response was, "Well, I didn't want to hurt his feelings." As you can imagine, she brought up this issue repeatedly until the end of all communication with her.

Chapter

13 The Seven Steps of Separating From Maureen

L et me take you back to my driveway where, three years ago, I stood slack-jawed and dumbfounded as Maureen departed for Mexico, leaving me with a "honey-do" list four miles long. Maureen couldn't have been more polite and good-natured prior to her trip to Mexico. She had begun **Step One** of the relationship destruction process by temporarily gaining my trust and talking me into our infamous business venture. She baited her hook with an intriguing business proposition, and she seasoned it with flattering comments about my artistic abilities, sense of style and people skills.

When she returned, her demeanor had changed completely. We were no longer a team. Quickly, she went into **Step Two** of the process. She talked about *her* business and how *she* wanted it handled, even though she had originally insisted that we be fifty-fifty partners. When I managed to interject an idea, Maureen's eyes glazed over like the eyes of a drug addict. She didn't want to hear anything that I had to say. As soon as I paused, she would pick up right where she had left off, enumerating the changes and additions *she* wanted to make to *her* business.

Our relationship was changing, and changing rapidly, but at that time I didn't understand why. I continued to do what I needed to do on my end, and then Maureen would call and say, for example, "I want to buy a warehouse to put our stuff in." There wasn't anything to put in a warehouse except for a few boxes, but I started looking for space.

Virtually each and every day, she had a new idea and a new list of tasks for me to accomplish. We were straying further and further from our original course. "I want to open a shop and sell beautiful things," she said one day. "I want to fill a warehouse and sell it to the trades," she said on another occasion. She had me so off track that at one point I even suggested we get into the food distribution business.

As her story persistently changed, I tried to keep my cool.

"What do you want to do now?" I would ask while biting my bottom lip and drawing blood.

After careful contemplation and a lot of running in circles, I called Maureen to stress the importance of concentrating on our original investment. I continued to impress upon her why we needed a business plan and an outline before we looked into a warehouse.

Admittedly, I probably contributed to the onset of **Step Three** by reminding her that we hadn't sold any of our products yet, so a warehouse seemed a bit premature. Because I'm sure she viewed this as a criticism of her business instincts, she attacked mine.

"You don't understand business," she barked. 'We need to invest money and buy more, more, more!"

I got the distinct impression that she'd just had a marathon phone conversation with the brother-in-law who was no doubt trying to protect her from the wicked partner. "You can't take effective criticism, Christina, and I'm not sure this is going to work. Furthermore," she continued smugly, "I think you are very controlling."

There it was, as plain as the pimple on her nose: my way out! Did I take it? No. What I should have said was, "You're right. I know it isn't going to work."

Then I should have gotten the hell out of there. But, I didn't. I stayed and hoped that things would change for the better.

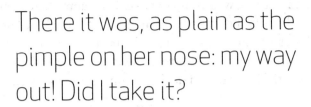

There it was, as plain as the pimple on her nose: my way out! Did I take it?

We continued to prepare for the upcoming trade show, despite being ill-equipped and still not on the same page as partners. I could feel a dark cloud looming over me. It didn't help when a desert plant with razor sharp leaves cut into my leg while I was getting into my car, all the while telling Maureen how excited I was about the trade show. Even the plant was trying to warn me to wake up. I still have a scar on my leg to this day.

My spirits were temporarily lifted when a woman at the trade show placed a large order and wanted to do a writeup about our products in a magazine. When Maureen returned to our booth after preening in the bathroom yet again, I told her the good news. I also told Maureen about the new product line that the woman had suggested—it was actually one that Maureen and I had already discussed and planned on adding in the future. Something that should have been a promising validation of our efforts turned into something ugly right before my eyes. Maureen dove headfirst into **Step Four**.

"That is what I said we needed to do in the beginning! If we'd already made the product, we could have sold more at the show. This always happens to me! I ran my own business once and listened to others and it went under. I should have known to listen to my own instincts!" she ranted. Then she proceeded to malign my product displays.

"Do you know how much it drives me crazy the way you arranged that?" she snipped. She was off on her "poor me" tangent and nothing was going to make her happy. Later, she called Jared while she was sitting in our booth to whine some more. "God, someone is going to steal our idea! Someone liked it and took a sample and they are going to go home and copy it! I came up with this idea and now someone is going to steal it!"

This dialogue went on for hours while the poor guy was on his honeymoon.

How was I feeling at the time? I wanted to say, "Man, do you need some serious help!" The people in the trade show booth next to us kept shooting me sympathetic looks.

"Stop telling me to calm down!" She spat on the way back to our hotel. She continued to pick at a pimple on her chin—which in her case is a sure sign that she is not about to let something go. I certainly wasn't looking forward to dining with her that evening.

I'll bet Rod Sterling himself never imagined something so twisted.

Maureen indulged in a bit too much alcohol during dinner, so I paid the price when we returned to our hotel room later that night. Drunk on top of ornery, she lapsed into her past and spoke fanatically of a former boyfriend. She began flailing her arms and legs on the bed while screaming about being victimized by her past love. Before I knew it, hotel security was at the door, responding to complaints that someone was being beaten. I'll bet Rod Sterling himself never imagined something so twisted.

Later, I laid down on my own hotel bed in the dark, expressionless and void of all emotion. A tiny voice in my head cried a sheepish *Help*. I had three more days of the show to go.

Just when I thought I had witnessed enough mental illness to last me a lifetime, I had to experience it all over again the following morning on the way *back* to the trade show. Maureen and I passed a store that sold clothing for young women. Painted on the storefront window was the silhouette of a naked woman with her breasts jutting forward, her back arched and her legs spread apart. I stopped in my tracks, thinking that the image was pretty damn provocative. I felt that it was promoting promiscuity for young girls. Being the mother of a teenage girl, such attention-grabbing advertising blew me away, and I let out a "Wow." That's all the provocation Maureen required.

"Christina, you don't understand business. Sex sells and I should know! Have you ever been to a car show? Well, half-naked women are walking around everywhere. I'm a business-woman and I should know. You are such a prude!" She ranted and raved as if I had just criticized a fine work of art. Sex might sell, but I didn't want my teenage daughter buying it.

The last day of the trade show **Step Five** emerged in all its glory. I felt like Scrooge waiting for the last ghost. Mother Teresa was hit by the two-by-four as Maureen sat in a restaurant pureeing her food and saying, "What do you want, Christina? I'll buy you out and even pay for the hotel and your plane ticket."

You've heard the rest of this particular story. She was handing me a way out on a silver platter, and this time I took it.

While flying home, Maureen had a seat across the aisle from me. She talked pleasantly to the man next to her for the entire flight. She acted as if nothing had happened. I felt sick to my stomach. I couldn't wait to get home to my family.

But the plane ride home wasn't the last of Maureen. After arriving home, **Step Six** began to unfold. I waited patiently for the merchandise from the trade show to be returned to my home. When the delivery truck pulled up, I asked him to follow me to Maureen's home to drop off the boxes because she was going to buy me out. Thinking logically, I knew there was no point having her come to my home to retrieve the boxes.

Maureen's daughter was home at the time, so she opened the garage door, and the deliveryman dropped off the boxes. Later on, I made an appointment to meet Maureen at the bank to sign off as a partner and to collect my half of the investment. When I called to see if she was ready, her response was, "I don't have any money. I don't know what you want from me, Christina!"

Then she hit me with yet another two-by-four out of left field. She told me how "traumatized" her daughter had been when I showed up at her door with the delivery driver. She said that her daughter knew about the disintegration of our partnership and that she was highly uncomfortable with me standing in their garage the day of the delivery. This is seriously doubted, given I had practically helped raise her daughter when Maureen was distracted for long spells.

Step Seven, of course, soon followed. Maureen moved on to her next victim. This one, I heard, was taken for thousands of dollars.

There's no need to remember the seven steps in great detail; just look for inconsistencies in words and actions, and never assume that you will be treated any differently from others in the Wacko's past.

I'm not the only one in my family to be lured in by a W3's baited hook.

My husband and I (and even our son, Alex) had the extreme displeasure of dealing with a W3 as a family. We met a man who really exemplified three of the W3 traits: he was self-absorbed; emotionally unstable; and fanatic about holding grudges. We were fooled at first, but we had learned from *my* past mistakes with Wackos! Here's the story:

"Coach Bully" was a W3 volcano on the verge of erupting. My husband and I just didn't know it at the time. As newcomers to his crowd, we were impressed with his sparkling personality and the vastness of his generosity. He was a wealthy man who seemed to spare no expense on the people in his life. He surrounded himself with a posse of people he'd known for years. They got together on a regular basis to eat, drink and laugh. Anyone with a support system of this magnitude had to be worth knowing and befriending, right? That's what we thought, too.

Everyone called him Coach because he had often volunteered to coach the various athletic teams on which his son played. His devoted followers thought that he was a saint for sacrificing so much of his personal time to help the kids. Knowing what I know now, I think his desire to coach didn't stem from his love of children or sports, but rather his craving to control others. And let's face it; young people are easy targets. So, for that matter, are adults when they fail to watch, look and listen.

Looking back on things now, it was quite surreal (and downright creepy) the way everyone danced to his tune. His minions were just too amenable, too adoring. They were like *Stepford* friends.

"I don't let many people into my group, but I like you two," Coach whispered to me while seeming to leer at my breasts. He said it like he was doing us some big favor. In hindsight, I realize those lemmings were the only people he *would* have anything to do with because he could control all of them. They had perfected the art of being hosts and seemed so far beyond being in touch with their own personal realities. Coach's life had become their reality—as if they had been brainwashed. How fortunate we felt to be added to this gang of drones! What in the world were we thinking? Coach clearly had us snowed.

Looking back on things now, it was quite surreal the way everyone danced to his tune.

As our relationship with Coach continued, so did Coach's obsession with our family. Coach was determined to turn Ched and me into his cohorts, and he thought he had the perfect carrot to dangle in front of Ched. He asked Ched to come and run his "multi-million dollar companies," but Ched, who was running his own successful business, didn't take the bait. Something about Coach Bully's demeanor changed immediately after Ched gently and politely declined his offer. Coach seemed more determined than ever to win over Ched, and he wouldn't let the subject drop.

We were all enjoying a football game, sandwiched together in a crowded stadium, when Coach repeated his job offer—a gesture that was "unheard of" in his lopsided, controlling world. Man, he was used to getting what he wanted—tout de suite!

"I *never* ask anyone twice to come to work for me," he seethed, straining to control his tone. His face turned beet red. While this happened, I again felt him staring at my breasts with his wife sitting right next to him. She reached over and gently told him to stop.

Two weeks later, after Ched rejected Bully's *third* job offer, Ched and I decided that we were both too uncomfortable to continue with the friendship. Coach was starting to give both of us the heebie-jeebies, so we listened to our guts and started coming up with excuses not to attend gatherings with him.

Apparently, our ability to resist Coach's attempts at manipulation caused his self-esteem to falter. Instead of facing rejection and moving on, he decided to wield control over a more vulnerable segment of society: young teens.

Alex had several friends on one of Coach's teams, and the stories we heard from Alex were shocking. Coach had turned his obsessive behavior toward one of Alex's best friends, Seth, who was also one of the team's youngest, most talented players.

Coach Bully tried to re-inflate his ego by belittling Seth and by blaming the kid for things he didn't do. Coach didn't listen when the other teammates owned up to the disruptive behavior to get Seth off the hook. "I don't care!" the man would yell back at them. "Seth, do ten laps now!" He yelled at him relentlessly during practices and in the classroom sessions. The kid ran all the laps and did all the pushups that Coach threw at him. The Marines would have been proud!

Seth refused to give in to the grueling treatment. Nor would he give up. Coach didn't like that one bit.

He talked to teachers about Seth and hovered over Seth in the school and in the parking lot. He even went to a school play that Seth was participating in and sat in the front row with his arms crossed against his chest in disapproval. Whatever his motive, the ploys failed to work. People continued to think the kid was funny and a downright talented athlete.

The other teammates couldn't understand Bully's irrational and over-the-top anger toward Seth and would constantly ask Seth why he put up with it. In fact, *Bully* finally asked Seth why he was putting up with it. Seth's response? His love of the game.

One night during a classroom session about game techniques he asked Seth what he would do in a particular situation. Coach didn't like the answer and kicked him out of the class.

The other students were stunned.

"But, Coach, I would have answered your question the same way," replied a brave teammate.

"I don't care," Bully grumbled, with no further explanation.

Later on, Coach found Seth waiting for his mother to pick him up and told him he was off the team for the season. "I never liked you from the first time I met you," Bully growled. The volcano had erupted.

Don't try being rational with a W3. You can't reason with the unreasonable.

Coach lost his coaching gig once the school administrators learned what happened, though it's sad commentary that no one in the community bothered to inform school leaders earlier that this guy was out of control. Admittedly, that includes me and my own family.

Just remember that when you are dealing with a W3, they will hold a grudge for the rest of their lives. Maureen is still out there bashing me to this day even though she has moved on to her third or fourth victim.

The lesson to be learned here: if you are a teenager or even an adult, don't try being rational with a W3. You can't reason with the unreasonable. Once you witness such immature, fanatical behavior and realize you're with a W3, move on. It's a matter of self-preservation—a topic you will learn about in Chapter 17.

Teenagers are vulnerable targets for the Wackos of the world. If you've got a son, daughter, niece or nephew who may be dealing with a Wacko, check out my tips for teens in Chapter 18.

When dealing with a W3, you must remain calm and try not to get defensive. If you engage in her drama, you are giving her exactly what she wants: center stage. W3s thrive on pandemonium, and they love gabbing on the phone and spreading their stories of constant chaos. They are utterly self-absorbed and have no control over their emotions. Remember, even though W3s don't listen to what you say, they *do* learn all of your imperfections and retain the information for Step Four of the relationship destruction plan. They hold grudges and carry out vendettas.

Some extra advice for this type would be to watch how your children react to them. Young children, especially those with a stable home life, will act like the wrong end of a magnet when they're around negative energy; they won't connect. My smallest child wouldn't get near the last W3 in my life. If only she had had the vocabulary at the time to explain to me what she was sensing!

The only Wacko level that supersedes a W3 is, naturally, a Wacko 4 (W4). Most Wackos never reach this stage inhabited by those few who are predisposed to abuse. On paper, the differences that separate a Level 4 from earlier Wacko incarnations may seem slight; to witness a W4 wielding these traits, however, is chilling.

The W4 Level represents the culmination and refinement of all Wacko traits. The self-absorption, the manipulation, the defense mechanisms are fine-tuned to the point of being difficult to detect by others. W4s are excellent actors and actresses, capable of camouflaging their devious ways. Whereas W3s purposely drop trails of breadcrumbs and thrive on notoriety, W4s simply seek to blend in to better cover their trails of destruction.

> The Level 4 Wacko represents the culmination and refinement of all Wacko traits.

The watch, look and listen technique is highly effective with the first three Wacko levels, but this particular method won't help you initially detect W4s. Most people will only realize that they're involved with a W4 *after* the Wacko has done something openly heinous or despicable—at which point the damage has already been done. W4s are not transparent; they don't drop hints. He might manipulate, belittle and conspire—just like a W3—but he will do so in a way that is almost impossible to sense. A W4 can fool just about anyone into believing she is someone she isn't. These are the people you read about or see on the news who get caught after decades of abusing loved ones or pocketing company dollars. They fool adults and children—especially the insecure.

So, is there anything you *can* do to protect yourself from this type? The best advice I can give you is to trust your instincts. If your gut tells you that your new acquaintance does not seem genuine, listen to your inner voice and don't let your guard down. Be prepared to walk away the minute your suspicions are validated.

I had nothing but my instincts to rely upon one weekend when we hosted someone we had never met. A friend of mine had asked if someone she knew could stay with us for a weekend conference. The man was supposedly doing some groundbreaking work in the healing field, and I thought he'd be interesting to meet. Besides, I trusted my friend so I didn't think there'd be a problem. As you can guess, there was—but it was intangible at the time.

The minute I met the man, the hair on my arms stood up. As cordial as he was, I didn't like him although I couldn't put my finger on why. Trust me; it wasn't the holes in his socks or his unusually hairy body. I kept a close eye on my children and immediately washed the sheets in the guest room and sterilized the bathroom after his departure to calm my case of the willies. I had to erase any trace of his existence in my home.

Three weeks later my friend called and asked my opinion of him. I was honest with her, and she told me that my instincts were accurate. She found out soon after the conference that he was a dishonest egomaniac who mentally abused those around him. This particular situation validated my theory about sniffing out W4s: If it feels weird, it is weird—no matter how much money the person makes or how he dresses or what he might contribute to society. Don't be fooled.

And The Award for Best Performance Goes to...

A W4 can act his or her way into and out of any situation with a flawless performance. He can paste the right expression on his face, strike the right pose and say just the right things to convince anyone of his sincerity. A W4 will strike with light-ning speed and, of course, when there are few or no witnesses. The strike—whether verbal or physical—will leave the victim stunned. It's typical for a victim in this situation to point a finger at the abuser and say in astonishment, "You just bit me!" Don't expect the Wacko to own up to any wrongdoing. The Wacko will calmly and effortlessly share his version of the events with anyone caught up in the drama. He will be so convincing that everyone will believe that the victim is actu-ally the one lying. W4s are psychotic but intelligent—make no mistake about that. A W4 is actually exceedingly intelligent with an infinite memory. Most of us would trip over our lita-nies of lies, but W4s remember all of their tall tales because they need them for their acts.

My friend Sheila was unfortunate enough to marry a W4. Her former husband, Phil, (whom you will learn much more about soon) once was pulled over for speeding. The police officer asked Phil for his license, and Phil silently dug into his pocket and mentally prepared his act. He began by adopting the right facial expression. He quivered his bottom lip and made tears well up in his eyes.

"Certainly, officer," he choked in a smooth Southern drawl with a huge, fictitious lump in his throat.

"I'm going to have to give you a ticket for going twenty miles over the speed limit," the officer sternly told him.

He looked at the officer and said, "Well, I'm so sorry for driving so fast but I just got a call from the hospital informing me my mother had a ... a heart attack!" He burst into tears and ran his fingers through his highlighted hair and turned up the drama meter. Phil buried his face in his hands, howling and shaking his head.

The officer stood in complete shock, probably racked with guilt, and watched this poor man come unglued in front of him. "I'll tell you what," the officer declared while standing straight and tall, "You go on and get to the hospital, but you need to drive calmly and at the speed limit. I hope everything will be all right. Good luck."

"Thank you, officer, and God bless you!" Phil called out the window, wiping his tears away. Phil's two young sons witnessed that flawless performance, and they sat in the car flabbergasted as their father dried his eyes and started laughing.

Chapter 15 Characteristics of a Wacko 4

O nce you've taken a close look at the characteristics of a W4, it will be obvious how the traits of earlier Wacko levels progress if unacknowledged or untreated to Wacko Level 4. For instance, all Wackos desire to control others, and in the earliest stages of W1, this is attempted mainly through words. In higher Wacko levels, this sense of control is achieved through emotional or psychological manipulation. When these relatively surreptitious methods of control are no longer enough to satisfy the Wacko, this behavior may enter a darker realm where it borders or becomes physically abusive, or it may start involving the manipulation of people surrounding the intended victim.

The same goes for a Wacko's desire to always be an attention-hound. As this trait progresses, Wackos will do almost anything to remain in the spotlight. You'll just have to read about it to believe it.

The following characteristics hold true for most W4s:

It's All About Control
I Must Be the Center of Attention
It's All a Game
I'm Threatened by the Powerful
I'm Entitled to Pry

It's All About Control

W4s must control everyone in and around their lives; this is the solitary most important thing necessary for a W4's existence. Wielding their power over other people makes these über Wackos feel safe. Being in command at all times is as essential as breathing to W4s. They can do it in their sleep, while awake, telepathically and psychically. Any time a W4 feels like he or she might be losing control over someone, he may resort to physical or mental abuse. But remember what separates a W4 from his earlier counterparts: a W4 will make sure that no one else is listening or looking when the Wacko behavior surfaces. A W4 is an expert at preserving his or her image of being a stellar human being. Talk about a distorted sense of supremacy.

> Being in command at all times is as essential as breathing to Wacko 4s.

Sheila's former husband, Phil, (whom I mentioned earlier) always tried to control her. At first, she found his behavior annoying but otherwise harmless. As the years passed and her resistance to his attempts at control remained the same, Phil's frustration grew. His suppressed anger eventually erupted, and he physically assaulted her twice. There weren't any witnesses; however, the second time he raised his hand to her she was smart enough to file a police report. Sheila eventually asked Phil for a divorce, which temporarily knocked him off balance. Once he regrouped, he was ready to abuse again.

Not wanting to risk jail time for another physical assault, he decided to really hit Sheila where it would hurt most.

Phil paraded his debonair façade into the courthouse like a proud peacock with his highly-paid attorney. Before Sheila knew it, the doofus had exploited her deficiency of funds (a previous car accident had left her bed-ridden, broke and temporarily unable to physically care for the children) and managed to get full custody of both children. He walked out of chambers smirking like the Grinch Who Stole Christmas. For a ten-year period he used his "I have sole custody" decree to prevent Sheila from having any kind of substantial relationship with her children.

He did everything within his power to keep the children away from her. He installed call block on his phone so the children couldn't even say good night to their mother, and he gave them each a cell phone to use when they were with their mother so that he could call them any time. He once called the kids and told them to tell Sheila that they were taking a walk. Phil then picked them up and drove them back to his house. Phil didn't care that legally it was Sheila's weekend. He knew she didn't have enough money to take him to court. "She is stalking me," he told police officers, lawyers and teachers.

Sheila made desperate attempts to spend her legally appointed time with her children. She allowed her temper to rise to the boiling point (which haunts her to this day), as Phil would stand by calmly and ask any onlookers, "Do you see what I have to deal with?"

Phil lived in a mansion; he owned two businesses and a considerable amount of land. Yet he tried to put Sheila in jail for delinquent child support payments. When the judge asked Phil why he was taking such drastic measures over a little bit of money, which he clearly didn't need, Phil fed her a bunch of baloney about wanting his kids to respect the law. The judge dismissed his motion and his attitude with her observation: "It appears Mr. 'Grinch' that it's all about control for you." That was the only time in seventeen years that someone agreed with Sheila. The judge ordered Phil and Sheila to arrange a schedule that had to be honored.

It didn't end there. Phil refused to honor Sheila's court-ordered visitation dates. The two ended up in court a year later. During that time, Shelia spent hours upon hours gathering documents from doctors and other healthcare professionals proving his abusive parenting. Sheila couldn't afford an attorney, so she did all of the legwork. Her efforts resulted in a "Phil file" three inches thick. He had approved anti-depressant drugs for their young child and even took him to an amusement park to ride roller coasters soon after the child was struck by a car and suffered a massive head injury. Since Shelia couldn't afford an attorney, she sent the documentation directly to the judge to read before the hearing.

The hearing began, and there on the judge's bench was the documentation. Sheila was lucky to get a word in edgewise as she tried to defend herself against Phil and his high-priced lawyer. It appeared as if the judge didn't have time to read the documentation because, in the end, Sheila lost the few rights that she still had and is lucky if she can see the kids a few times a year.

Phil was unyielding in his pursuit to obliterate Sheila's existence without blatantly killing her. If their children saw their father for what he really was, they didn't show it. In fact, money appeared more important to them than their mother—not surprising given how they saw their father use his funds to exact revenge and lord over people. They also stood by his side during their college years, which their father fully financed.

Phil wasn't satisfied just manipulating the kids, either. His hunger to control every aspect of Sheila's life was insatiable. He tried to influence and manipulate any member of the community who would listen to his side of the story. One of his targets was the school their children attended. One by one, he convinced teachers and parents alike that Sheila was irritating and impossible to handle.

> Phil was unyielding in his pursuit to obliterate Sheila's existence without blatantly killing her.

For ten years, Sheila endured cruel looks and the cold shoulder treatment during school events. "I encourage all of you as parents to work with and support your children," Phil, president of the PTA, said to his loyal followers during a meeting. He was handsome and exuded self-confidence, and his six-foot, two-inch frame commanded attention. The teaching staff watched adoringly and took note of their charismatic leader while Sheila shrank into her seat in the back of the room feeling like a skunk in a perfumery.

I Must Be the Center of Attention

Like all Wacko levels, a W4 will do anything and *everything* to be the center of attention. Being center-stage is vital to his existence. Anyone who steals the limelight, whether inadvertently or intentionally, will quickly become the Wacko's target. Insults will fly. Lies will be fabricated. War will be waged, calmly and underhandedly. Once the accidental scene-stealer has been vanquished, the Wacko will regain the lead role. A Wacko might feign an illness to get attention or simply exaggerate current events in his life to refuel everyone's admiration and fascination with him.

You can count on never receiving any form of acknowledgement or recognition from a W4 for anything, however extraordinary, you accomplish. What you will hear repeatedly is praise for the accomplishments of others. The Wacko knows you are longing to hear praise and approval from him and such denial is part of their ploy to remain in control of a relationship.

I had just finished my first draft of this book when I was invited to a cocktail party. I suspected, based upon stories I'd heard about him, that one of the other guests fit my W4 mold to a T. At the party, I decided to test my theory regarding this particular guest, so I made a point of striking up a conversation with him. I introduced myself and asked the Wacko how he knew the hosts—the usual party ice-breaker. I didn't need to utter another word after that. After listening to this particular Wacko speak endlessly about himself and how wonderful he thinks he is, I managed to interject that I had just written a book. Without skipping a beat, he continued to go on about a recent promotion and the "fast track" that he was most certainly on at the bank. No way he was giving up his coveted center-stage position!

It's All A Game

Nothing gives a W4 more gratification then manipulating the innocent and unsuspecting. Wackos crave control like kids crave sugar. W4s are master manipulators who torment their hapless prey like my dog Ben tortures colossal Arizona spiders with his oversized paws.

A few years ago, I watched with morbid interest as Ben took his wide paw and stomped on a tarantula. Had he wanted to kill it outright, I'm certain he would have; Ben just wanted to toy with it. Ben plopped down with his head between his two front legs, his nose just inches away from his victim, and waited patiently for the spider to recover from the initial blow. Ben's ears were pointed forward as he watched the tangled mass of legs and fuzz with genuine interest. When the spider began to wobble around like a drunkard, Ben got up and repeated the same scenario. Eventually, Ben tired of the repetition and started grabbing the spider with his teeth and flipping it up into the air, all the while sneezing and snuffing from the spider's attempts to bite his tongue. Finally, the spider didn't get up; Ben had slowly killed it, but that didn't stop him from waiting patiently for the next victim to come along.

Wacko 4s are master manipulators who torment their hapless prey like my dog Ben tortures colossal Arizona spiders with his oversized paws.

W4s may not actually sprawl out on sidewalks waiting to swat their next victims in the head (although maybe some do!), but the primary goal is the same as Ben's, and the outcome will be the same—metaphorically speaking. A W4 will repeatedly pick at a victim's soul until the victim no longer fights back. It's all a game to a W4, just like it is to Ben. The Wacko is just trying to show the world who is in control.

Most of the games that Wackos will play are mind games, which are a tad advanced for Ben, but once again the similarities in the goals and outcomes are undeniable.

I grew up with a friend, Tracy, whose father we now know was a W4. When she and her two other siblings were young teenagers, their father treasured pitting them against each other—all behind the scenes. I'm confident it was absolutely side-splitting for him to stand back and watch everyone turning against each other, spying on each other and reporting back information to him. They all did this to gain his acceptance. The most wretched part about the whole situation, from my standpoint, was knowing that Tracy and her siblings didn't have a clue that they were being played. Frank would purposely try to cause jealousy, resentment and anger among his children.

"This one has the brains; this one has the looks; and this one has the personality," he would say in front of all of the children. I can only theorize that Frank did this so that he would feel needed and in control; if the kids couldn't turn to each other for love and support, they would turn to him. And as long as they were coming to him with their problems, they weren't forming their own self-supporting posse whose actions he couldn't dictate. Tracy wanted so desperately to get along with her siblings, but she was fighting an uphill battle. Frank kept stoking the fires of sibling rivalry in his perverse attempts to control them.

One of Frank's other favorite games was to reward one child for sharing secrets about another. When it served him, Frank would repeat these entrusted confidences just to prove to his brood that he knew everything that they did, so they'd better do no wrong. Money was usually the means through which he rewarded and punished, so money became a substitute for love, in the hearts of his children.

Tracy has been in therapy, but to this day, she doesn't like to talk on the phone because all of her calls were listened to while she was growing up.

Tracy and her siblings grew up never having learned to be there for each other. They also learned not to trust each other and, most tragic of all, they never knew the joy of loving each other. Frank got the job done.

What really saddens Tracy now is recalling the times when her father would try to make them feel guilty for not getting along with each other. "Why does this always happen? All I want is for my children to get along," he would mock.

It's all a game to a W4. If you're old enough to resist, don't play along.

I Feel Threatened by the Powerful

W4s love to view themselves as kings and queens and everyone else as mere pawns in a chess game of life. Anyone who tries to counter a Wacko's warped game strategy is viewed as a threat. Even if that "anyone" is an offspring of the Wacko's.

Children raised by Wackos are certainly the most unfortunate Wacko victims of all.

I once became acquainted with a man whom I later surmised was raised by a W4. I thought he had a tremendous presence and stood out in any crowd. What baffled me was that Darrell seemed completely unaware of his power, and he had a serious lack of self-esteem. The more I got to know him, the more I understood why.

His mother, Alice, always put him down—sometimes blatantly and sometimes subtly. All he knew was that after being in her presence he felt deflated and depressed. He didn't quite know why until he started to really listen—not just to his mother but also to himself. He quickly realized that Alice cut and jabbed because his achievements made her feel threatened. She never beamed with pride; she teemed with resentment. He also realized that when his mother wasn't around to insult him, he found ways to insult himself. It's all he knew: he didn't deserve the spotlight; she did.

Children raised by Wackos are certainly the most unfortunate Wacko victims of all.

Darrell's mother never commented when Darrell got a job or promotion or even after he opened his own business. She would compliment anyone but her own son. When he rose to a vice presidential position, he felt elated. Alice's only comment was, "Oh, how did you talk them into that?"

How could Darrell not have a poor self-image after processing put-down after put-down for most of his life?

She criticized any flaw she could find when she visited Darrell's home. She was jealous of his wife, his house and his cars. She wasn't about to acknowledge any facet of Darrell's life that spelled success. When Darrell closed his business to get out of the rat race, his mother's response was, "I told you to sell it years ago!"

Prying is My Middle Name

To a W4, no information is sacred. No topic is taboo. A W4 will openly inquire about your income, the price of your house, the cost of your car, your spouse's salary, your parents' annuities and so on. A W4 will pry into personal information not for curiosity's sake but for survival's sake—they need this information to feel in control. The more information, the better, just in case it will prove useful at a later date.

I don't know about you, but I think most people, me included, feel caught off-guard when someone boldly asks for private information. We're so shocked that what do we do? We spill those private details. I'm always angry with myself when I'm in this position and the words the Wacko is looking for just pop right out of my mouth. I feel violated by the Wacko's question, but at the same time I'm disappointed with my inability to tell the Wacko to butt out.

Typically with W4s, prying doesn't stop with a verbal inquisition. This type will look through your desk drawer when you leave the office or look over your shoulder and read what's on your computer screen. She will glance over your mail on the counter at home—mentally scanning return addresses for any useful information; she will eavesdrop on your conversations and mentally record and store the information indefinitely. She will not hesitate to use this pilfered personal information if backed into a corner.

We all know busybodies—those overly curious, abundantly available people who always seem to know everyone else's business. A W4 is different. The neighborhood Nosey Nellie just likes to know what's going on; a W4 wants to know to strengthen their verbal munitions.

I've come to the conclusion that a W4 would hold a séance to pry more information from the dearly departed if the Wacko thought the information might be useful.

Chapter

16 Document Everything

I f you are courageous enough to try to expose a W4,
document everything. Without documentation you have
nothing. Trying to expose a W4 is like trying to get out of
quicksand. The harder you struggle, the harder the Wacko
will work to make sure you sink.

Sheila, for example, struggled to make people believe her
side of the story, and she had documents—including a police
report—to prove her ex-husband was a malevolent man. But
Phil was so convincing that people bought his explanation
for everything. The harder she tried to expose Phil, the more
desperate she looked. A W4 will not, under any circumstances, allow his or her true perverted self to be revealed
and will fight to the end to protect his image. The longer you
stay in the relationship, the more in jeopardy you are of either
losing your God-given spirit for living or losing your life altogether. Documentation might give you some mental leverage
and confidence, if nothing else.

Another acquaintance of mine learned the hard way what
it's like to work for a W4. In this case, documenting
the Wacko's comments could have definitely given her
a mental advantage.

"Are you always this uptight during an interview?" her
future employer asked, unnerving her with his candor

while shamelessly picking his nails. His attitude was as smug as his hair was thin. He crossed his legs to reveal a sock-less foot in a high-end loafer and plucked imaginary lint from his expensive trousers.

"Are you always this uptight during an interview?" her future employer asked, unnerving her with his candor while shamelessly picking his nails.

Tina sat at the table at the outdoor café, talking with the owner of a head-hunting firm. He recruited for all the big construction companies in Atlanta and was looking for an assistant to run the office, answer the phones and help him recruit. They had agreed to a lunchtime interview to accommodate both of their schedules.

Tina was tense, to say the least, and she was embarrassed that she'd let it show. Her spine felt wooden and her jaw ached from clenching her teeth. Interviews had always made her nervous, but this one was especially stressful. For starters, her first impression of the man sitting across the table from her was not a positive one. He stared at her face, her breasts, her legs; you name it; he stared at it. She had the distinct feeling that he could sense that she was hiding something. She wasn't hiding a personal situation so much as waiting for the right moment to explain her actions. He seemed to enjoy watching her squirm. She had the eerie sensation that the table separating them was starting to shrink, just like her self-confidence. She wanted to get the heck out of there—and fast.

Then, he popped the question: He asked her to work for him. Getting out of her current job with dignity was Tina's top priority. She was living with her boss and the entire company knew it. She wanted to make a graceful exit and transition seamlessly into a new working environment. Tina was turned off by Will, but felt as though she was at his mercy. It was the most promising job prospect she'd found in months.

Most people would never consider sharing such intimate details of their current employment with a potential boss. But, in typical "host" fashion, Tina handed her personal dilemma to Will on a platter along with Carrs Water Crackers, aged cheddar cheese and Russian caviar. Her Mother Teresa syndrome compelled her to share too many details about her life, never expecting those details to be used against her.

Obviously, after hearing about Tina's predicament, Will made a low-ball offer that even host Tina just couldn't accept. Tina scurried from the restaurant like a skittish cat, her head hanging low in a combination of repulsion and humiliation.

Will had her phone number and called on a weekly basis to see if she had found a better offer. "How are things going over there?" he would whisper into the phone while calling her at work. He upped his offer to a salary plus commissions and she accepted. Tina kept telling me there was something creepy about the man but she just couldn't put her finger on it.

When Tina showed up for her first day of work, she was shocked to see a small, low-rent office in the heart of Buckhead, a tiny section of Atlanta. The windows overlooked the center of town near a hot spot restaurant. Tina knew she was in trouble after only a few hours. First, they were the only two employees in the 1,000-square-foot workplace. Second, and equally eerie, was the arrangement of the furniture: their desks were facing each other. No wonder he hadn't wanted to interview her in his office. He may have been a successful recruiter, but his "big company" act was all smoke and mirrors. Will's "big company" consisted of just one big ego.

"Here is a list of people to call and this is what you say," Will instructed Tina. "Make these calls, and do it all day long. If you get a recruit, you make a commission."

Tina expected Will to leave for meetings with clients, but instead, he spent 9 to 5 staring at every inch of her body. Every inch, that is, except what was concealed by her desk. Every time Tina looked up at her boss, he was staring at her. To get up and walk away from the protection of her desk was degrading. In addition to being foolish enough to sleep with the boss at her former job, Tina remained a babe in the woods when it came to understanding sexual harassment. She needed the money and went to work every day, even as things became more nauseating.

Tina expected Will to leave for meetings with clients, but instead, he spent 9 to 5 staring at every inch of her body.

As the months wore on, Will came up with new ways to harass her. He would look over at her and request sexual favors. Being a typical host, Tina would just chuckle and tell him to take a hike.

He would respond with, "Oh, you know I was just kidding." But she didn't believe a word of it.

Of course, the forced office intimacy worked both ways. Tina witnessed Will's phone calls to the IRS, beseeching them for a long extension because he supposedly didn't have enough money to buy shoes for his children. Like a typical W4, he was a great actor, she had to admit. She would listen to him brag about how he would tell his wife that he was going out for cigs, and instead, he would roam the streets near the Peachtree Café trying to pick up young girls. "I almost picked up this hot chick last night. My BMW really impressed her but she wouldn't get in," he would brag to Tina the next morning.

It didn't stop there, either. He would insist that Tina join him for lunch to discuss business, but instead, he would discuss his desire to kiss her, gradually inching himself toward her as she gradually inched away. He would even drive past his home to show her the renovations, which cost hundreds of thousands of dollars but yet he couldn't pay his taxes. The worst and most typical thing about this W4 was that he had a wife at home who thought he was an honorable man and good father to their girls.

In the end, Tina realized she would never see any of the commissions she had been promised. Will's explanation was that none of her recruits had worked out. In fact, Will was interviewing the recruits in the evenings after Tina had gone home. Tina estimated that Will had pocketed anywhere from $20,000 to $50,000 in commissions from the construction companies. Tina never received a cent. Wham! There went the two-by-four. Better late than never.

In a last-ditch effort to make the job worth her while, she asked Will if she could become a partner in his business.

That way, she figured, she could finally make some real money.

Reality was finally catching up with Will. His attempts to control every aspect of Tina's employment were eroding. He exploded and yelled, "Who do you think you are? I built this company by myself! And furthermore, I'm appalled that you would even consider this idea. You're fired!" He had had enough of Tina's rejections and needed to move on to a more promising victim.

Tina packed her things and eventually found a much better employer.

Are there some things Tina could have done differently? Certainly. But a W4 is hard to corner. My advice for anyone who is around a W4 is to document, document and document. There were many occasions when Tina could have recorded Will's abusive comments. He never would have seen the hand-held recorder she could have turned on when he was on a roll. Without tangible evidence, she was powerless. I encouraged her to call both the IRS and his wife, but, being a W4, he probably could have wriggled his way out of both situations. In either case, Will would probably paint Tina as a jealous, angry woman who was bitter about being fired. He would make himself out to be the victim. It was a losing battle.

As I've said before, if it doesn't feel right, then it isn't. It's just that simple. You don't need a reason; you just need to trust your instincts. Tina knew from the beginning that the situation didn't feel right. She learned some valuable lessons ... the hard way.

W4s are certifiable, but because they are some of the best actors and actresses out there, they are hard to catch in the act. They seek to control others at all costs, and they must be the center of attention. They obsess and they seek to possess. It won't do any good to have a heart-to-heart with a W4, because it's all a game to them. If you stand in your power with a W4, you will threaten him or her and you will become the Wacko's next target. W4s will pry into your personal endeavors and use this information against you if it's at all possible. If you suspect that you're in a relationship with a W4, your best option is to end the relationship and never look back. If that isn't possible, document everything that happens and share what you know with a trusted friend or family member.

When you meet someone else who has been victimized by a W4, believe what he or she is saying or at least acknowledge a red flag. These are some of the phrases that may signal that someone is involved with a W4: "I can't believe what he got away with!" "Nobody believes me, and they think he is perfect." "After everything she has done to me she still wants to hurt me more."

Our dog, Ben, whom I'm certain the local arachnids classify as a W4, eventually went after his next victim. He just didn't realize that he had met his match. The poor thing came home with porcupine needles all over his face. Be the thorn in a W4's side—stick it to them if you get a chance.

Chapter 17 A Final Word on Family

I know what some of you are thinking. You're thinking that most of these methods of extraction are easy to employ on Wackos with whom you aren't bound because of family ties or career choice. But if you're like Suzanne or Genevieve, and you've got a Wacko swinging from your family tree, the situation is a tad more complicated. Likewise, if the Wacko in your life shares a printer and a fax machine with you. Avoiding these Wackos often means sacrificing time with others you care about (as can be the case with family members) or risking your job performance if you're forced to interact with a Wacko at work.

Let's recall Suzanne, who had the unfortunate experience of growing up with a Wacko older sister. She was essentially trapped with a Wacko throughout her childhood. As an adult, she was forced to face her sister during family gatherings. We witnessed Suzanne making two critical errors. First, when Sarah swiped one of Suzanne's shirts without asking, Suzanne engaged. She let Sarah's behavior elicit a negative reaction, and that's exactly what Sarah wanted. Suzanne's other big mistake came later in life when she let her guard down at Sarah's barbecue. Suzanne eventually concluded that her sister was never going to change—a realization that changed Suzanne's life for the better.

Genevieve's situation was extra tricky. How do you tell your future husband that you find his mother's behavior offensive and unbearable? Genevieve let Wanda's comments get under her skin. She retreated into the nearest bathroom to cry. Genevieve engaged. Exactly the way Wanda had hoped she would. Genevieve's other mistake was that she didn't seek her husband's support early enough. Facing a Wacko truly is easier when you aren't doing it alone. Genevieve really needed her husband to be on her side. Men aren't mind-readers, for Pete's sake. She should have spelled things out for him—in capital letters.

Family matters. It's blood. That's why victims like Suzanne keep trying to jump every hurdle and smooth every wrinkle. And that's why distancing ourselves from Wacko family members poses such a distinctive challenge. We hate to give up on family. Trust me when I say that you aren't the one abandoning the relationship—that's already been done by the Wacko. What you're doing is saving your energy for mutually fulfilling relationships, and I've got some advice on just how to do that.

Self-Preservation Mode

Both Suzanne and Genevieve could have benefited greatly from adopting an attitude that I call "self-preservation mode." We touched on this topic briefly in Chapter 6 when we met Suzanne and her older sister and again when we witnessed what Genevieve endured with her mother-in-law. I developed this line of defense specifically for situations involving "unavoidable" Wackos.

Self-preservation mode is simply doing what you need to do to preserve your own well-being when you're forced to tolerate a Wacko. To be fully immersed in self-preservation mode, you must let go of any imaginary "family obligations" you feel exist and see your Wacko kin for who and what they are. Or, in the case of a coworker, you must file away any notions that you have to be anything beyond businesslike with the Wacko sharing your office space. You don't have to be best friends with your sister, and you certainly don't have to be buddies with the schlump in the next cubicle. Do what you need to do to tolerate the Wacko, and don't engage in the Wacko's nonsense. Dismiss, dismiss, dismiss. Most victims of Wackos eventually wake up to this reality and segue subconsciously into self-preservation mode as a means of survival. Both Suzanne and Genevieve employed this technique after years of psychological abuse. It is my hope that by sharing this information, I will spare my readers a few years of similar torment.

Survivors of the Wacko experience can be some of the strongest humans among us.

Once you've entered into self-preservation mode, I cannot stress enough that you must maintain, maintain, maintain. Self-preservation mode can be tough to sustain when you're caught up in the joy of a holiday or a family wedding. No matter what the event, you cannot let your guard down. When your guard goes down, your risk factor goes up; your self-preservation stance may weaken; and you'll be left vulnerable to a Wacko's attack.

Survivors of the Wacko experience can be some of the strongest humans among us. We may be wounded birds, but we emerge empowered nonetheless. Mandy, who has grown to become a true and loyal friend of mine over the past two years, chose to open up to me about her W3 brother.

Just like Suzanne, Mandy had an abusive sibling who always managed to get away with his bad behavior. Although Mandy instinctively employed self-preservation mode early on, she let her guard down time and again later in life during family get-togethers, which enabled her brother to cause her more emotional distress. These lapses can be painful reminders that Wackos never change. Here's her story.

Mandy learned early in life that she wasn't going to have a healthy relationship with her brother. She stopped trusting him at the tender age of nine, when she caught fourteen-year-old Brody stealing money from her piggy bank. She had heard the unmistakable jangling of metal against stoneware coming from her room. She couldn't believe her eyes when she saw her brother holding her pink ceramic pig. True to her Mother Teresa form, she stood in the doorway of her room, her expression a mixture of disbelief and confusion, and did absolutely nothing. She opened her mouth to speak, emitting a fractured "squeak" sound.

Brody looked over his shoulder at her and seethed in a low tone between clenched teeth, "Don't even start with me, you little bitch."

He put the piggy bank down and brushed past Mandy, ramming into her tiny shoulder on his way out. Nothing was said. Nothing was done.

Brody's abusive behavior crossed all boundaries—emotional, psychological and physical. What she didn't realize was by not sticking up for herself and for what was right, she enabled her brother to continue to mistreat her (and most likely other people who tried to grow close to him as years went by).

Her silence served as a sanction of Brody's misdeeds and served as a bellwether of trouble to come.

Mandy recalled once sitting in a chair in the living room when she was caught off guard by her brother's sudden presence. She wrapped her tiny, frail arms around her bent legs, as if she were trying to disappear into the chair. Her tall, "dictator-in-the-making" teenaged brother walked into the room. He glared at her while whispering, "You are pathetic! You little drowned rat!" Mandy had a strong moment and responded with, "Oh really? Well someone could make a roadmap out of your eyebrows!" She realized instantly that she had made a huge mistake. A size twelve shoe shot its way toward her. Penned in the chair, she had nowhere to go. Within seconds, a black and blue goose egg bubbled up on her shin. Her brother had whispered his comments, but Mandy had yelled hers. Their mother's response was, "Mandy, I heard what you said to him. You shouldn't have said that." The Castro look-alike walked away unscathed and with his reputation intact.

This pattern went on and on and on.

Mandy grew up detesting her brother for how he treated her, but she was stuck—just plain stuck. Where was a little girl supposed to go? When her brother initially started bullying her, Mandy reported the behavior to her parents, who insisted that Mandy had done something to antagonize her brother. Wackos are terrific actors, and he sure had their parents hoodwinked.

In time, Mandy simply stopped telling her parents about the abuse, and she survived the mistreatment during her youth by disengaging. As Mandy matured, so did her emotions, and she realized that she didn't have to "love" her sibling just because they were conceived by the same two people. By not waging an emotional tug-o-war with herself over any so-called "family obligations," she set herself free to do anything she needed to do to survive without ever feeling guilty. She tried to avoid and ignore her brother as much as possible—a strategy that definitely got easier as she got older.

In time, Mandy simply stopped telling her parents about the abuse, and she survived the mistreatment during her youth by disengaging.

Her brother never outgrew his compulsion to create his own version of *Fear Factor* right in their home. He may have aged on the outside, but he never matured on the inside. Knowing that her cries for help would be unanswered, she ran for cover. She skipped breakfast to avoid Brody. After school, she ran to her room, locked the door and studied to avoid Brody. She made excuses at dinnertime to avoid Brody. If their parents left the two of them home alone, Mandy found a friend to stay with. "Can I spend the night at your house? I'll clean your bathrooms!"

Their parents never saw or never wanted to see what was happening because they bought Brody's explanation that his sister's reactions to his "playful teasing" were just plain absurd. "You've always been an emotional girl," their mother would say to Mandy. "Are you sure you aren't overreacting?"

By the time she reached adulthood, Mandy was painfully aware that no one was coming to her rescue. She would have to deal with this on her own.

Mandy went on to become an accomplished writer and was strong enough to accept her parents' denial of Brody's behavior. She would reach her thirties, however, before she was strong enough to dismiss her brother once and for all.

In the interim, Brody took every opportunity to belittle and shame Mandy during family gatherings. At a wedding, Brody tried to disparage Mandy in front of everyone for wearing a black dress. "This isn't a funeral! College didn't teach you much, did it?" he jibed. Like many hosts, Mandy thought she could handle the occasional encounter with her Wacko brother, but his behavior eventually took its toll.

A recent holiday season proved to be the breaking point for Mandy. The two-by-four finally hit hard enough to make her taste blood. During a family visit, her young son was being mischievous, and Brody the "parenting expert" spewed a stream of unfounded brutal remarks about Mandy's child. "That kid is a spoiled brat! Just leave him with me for a weekend, and I'll get him straightened out!"

That was it. She made the conscious choice right then and there to never again let herself be affected by Brody's comments. He could sputter all he wanted to, but as far as she was concerned, his words were worthless. She quietly and calmly strutted her tiny body over to her husband and said, "We are out of here." They picked up their son and left. You have read the book thus far. Nothing more to say.

Mandy learned the hard way—and after way too many years— to dismiss her brother's words and actions *completely*. No exceptions.

It took Suzanne, Genevieve and Mandy years to arrive at the same conclusion: that it's a waste of time and effort to try to salvage a meaningful relationship with a Wacko, even if that Wacko is a close family member. The best we can do is tolerate unavoidable Wackos when the circumstances require that we do so.

The following tips will help you employ and maintain self-preservation mode:

- First and foremost, put as much distance as you can between yourself and the Wacko, whether this distance is literal and physical or metaphorical and mental. If you're at a family gathering, plant your tush at the opposite end of the banquet table and stay involved in conversations with the non-Wackos surrounding you. For Mandy, physical distance between herself and Brody became paramount to her survival during the holidays. If you're forced to share an office space with a Wacko, keep yourself mentally distant by never sharing any personal information. Sometimes the best we can do is build a psychological barrier where no physical one exists.

- Confide in a trusted family member or your spouse. You'll experience a sense of relief when you uncork the pain and frustration that's been building up inside of you.

- Never let your guard down. Always watch, look and listen. If you even begin to think that the Wacko has changed his or her ways, remind yourself that Wackos rarely, if ever, change. Don't buy into his act.

- When you're confronted with rude behavior or a snide comment, dismiss, dismiss, dismiss. Nothing defuses a Wacko's spark faster than a would-be victim who simply refuses to react. A reaction is exactly what a Wacko wants. Don't give it to him.

- ▶ Keep an eye on your Caller ID. A ringing phone is not a demand; it's a request. No, it doesn't matter if it's Christmas Day, your birthday or other seemingly "legitimate" reasons for your Wacko sibling to be calling you. You are not obligated to talk to a person who's only going to cause you more pain. You're not being rude. You're preserving your own well-being.

- ▶ Even email correspondence is pointless with a Wacko. You're just opening up an electronic can of worms. My friend Sam just got out of a Wacko relationship. She sent a short and to-the-point email to exit the insanity. What she got in return was a four-page docudrama. She never read it. She disengaged by deleting.

We can't choose our family members, nor can we control their actions. But we can control our own reactions to the things these Wacko relatives say and do. Through self-preservation mode, we can protect ourselves from physical and emotional upset when we're forced to rub elbows with unavoidable Wackos. We can face these situations with dignity and preserve our own personal power by dismissing the Wacko's words and actions completely. No exceptions.

Y ou've just heard stories covering a wide range of relationship types, behaviors and even age groups. Wackos are everywhere, and they can show up at any point in our lives. If you've got a teenage son or daughter or perhaps a niece or a nephew, the stories about Suzanne and her sister, Sarah; Mandy and her brother, Brody; and Seth and Coach Bully might have struck a nerve. It's hard enough for a mature adult to handle a Wacko encounter, but for a teenager toting the typical teen baggage, the situation can be especially turbulent. You can help the young people in your life by arming them with the emotional tools they will need to tolerate any Wackos who wander through their lives.

First, some basic info to consider. There are two general settings in which teens might have run-ins with Wackos: within the home and outside the home. The teen may actually be living with a Wacko, as is the case with siblings or (God forbid) Wacko parents. Outside of the nuclear family, teens may have to deal with Wacko classmates, coaches, teachers and any other adult or child.

Within each of those two scenarios are two clear age groups: other teenagers and adults. How a teen should interact with a fellow teen who is a Wacko is different from how the teen should handle a Wacko adult.

All of this will be covered in great detail in my next book, *Winning Against the Wackos in Your Life ... for Teenagers.*

Until then, what follows is a brief summary of my advice for teens. Show this chapter to your favorite teenager and let him or her know that more help is on the way.

Harnessing Your Teen Power

Teens and Wackos make for a highly combustible combination for two main reasons: hormones and hormones. Teens are already so emotionally charged that their reactions to everyday circumstances seem greatly exaggerated. Throw a Wacko into the mix and a teen's emotions will likely spiral out of control. Because maintaining one's self-control is the secret to surviving Wacko encounters, teens are particularly vulnerable to having their power sucked dry by a Wacko.

Teens and Wackos make for a highly combustible combination for two main reasons: hormones and hormones.

Quite frequently, the first Wacko a young person faces is a sibling. So, where is a teen victim supposed to go? Out in the backyard to live in a tent? It's not unusual for the parents to ignore the teen's cries for help. Just an old-fashioned case of sibling rivalry, they assume. Wackos are scheming and iniquitous, and they are experts at getting away with it.

After numerous failed attempts to seek help from her parents, the teen host starts to feel isolated and helpless, while the Wacko's ego balloons. Quite frankly, I believe it was both Sarah's and Brody's drug to treat their younger siblings so badly. They got a high from it. Suzanne and Mandy, on the other hand, felt nothing but low. Teens are so susceptible to a Wacko's charms—so eager to feel accepted—that they let their guard down time and time again. Teens can defend themselves against Wackos by harnessing their personal power and hanging on to it for dear life. This is easier said than done, for obvious reasons. But the effort will pay off in the long run—trust me.

Here are some tips:

▶ First and most importantly, all the "Suzannes" out there need to accept that the Wacko in your life will **not** change. When you can accept this, **your** life will change. His or her character has been formed and she will hang on to her abusive ways till her death. She will **never** apologize or acknowledge the anguish, pain and emotional abuse she has caused you. Understanding this will set you free.

▶ You must never let your guard down. Never assume that the Wacko has changed.

▶ Exchange dialog with a Wacko only when or if you have to. I'm not saying to walk around with a chip on your shoulder, harboring anger and resentment. If you do, then you've helped your enemy achieve exactly what she set out to do. Just keep her at bay at all costs. Keep the conversations to a superficial minimum, and I guarantee your survival.

▶ **Never** try to defend yourself to a Wacko. She won't listen to what you have to say, and she doesn't care.

- Be in control, and control **your** anger. That's where the power comes in. I have passed this information on to my daughter and she uses it on me! I got angry with her for repeatedly not getting up on time for school, and I was looking for an argument. I was mad and wanted verbal fisticuffs. Instead of engaging in my anger, she became catatonic, and suddenly I felt powerless. She didn't react the way I wanted her to, so I had no one to fight with. Wow. The power coming from that moment was profound.

Remember the Jessica Method

Wackos like to use words to hurt people, so if you must, fight fire with fire. Because teens are big fans of snappy verbal comebacks, the Jessica Method is perfect for young people. The Jessica Method is the ideal way to maintain your dignity when reacting to a Wacko's undignified behavior. This method will help you stop a Wacko quickly without suffering any physical repercussions.

Keep in mind that the basis of the Jessica Method is to respond to a Wacko's ranting and raving with as few words as possible—five to seven words max.

Some examples of how to use the Jessica Method:

- If a Wacko says to you, "You are such a nothing. The world would be much better off without you," tilt your head to the side and say, "You might be right about that." That's six words, and she **will** be stopped in her tracks. You can use this brief, but effective, line when it comes to dealing with a controlling parent as well. Just try to tone it down a bit. Lower your head reverently and say, "You might be right about that." Tell her what she wants to hear and don't argue with her. Go to your room to cool off and to remind yourself to keep **your** anger under control.

- If a Wacko says, "Nobody likes you. That's why you don't have any friends," look her squarely in the eyes and say, "Huh." If she doesn't stop there and continues with something like, "Look at you! You act like you think you're Ivana Trump!" Continue to stare at her and say, "Really?" If she carries on, listen to what she says and give her an incredulous, "Wow!" Not only will this frustrate the Wacko, but also it might encourage her to take her Wacko ways elsewhere, which is ultimately the outcome you're seeking because you alone can't convert a Wacko to a wonderful human being.

- Another good line guaranteed to extinguish a Wacko's fire: "You shouldn't worry about it." This line works wonders when a Wacko is going on and on about a friend's "stuff" and is looking for an ally to join in the gossip session.

My heart goes out to teenagers who have to deal with Wackos. But you can live through the experience if you remember the basics: never let your guard down; never reveal personal information; record their behavior if at all possible; and accept your situation and know that you will have the upper hand if you can control *yourself*. That is the key to your survival over the next few years.

Forgive your enemy, but protect yourself. Don't carry the rage that the Wacko has brewed up inside you. Don't make her issues part of yours. When you can dismiss the Wacko's actions, you will get your power back.

We have, of course, just scratched the surface when it comes to the topic of teens and Wackos. Rest assured that more help is on the way soon.

Chapter 19 Let's Review

There's an abundance of helpful information tucked between the covers of this little book, but I'd wager that much of it is not entirely *new* information if you've had to share your life with various Wackos—as most of us have. In fact, I bet a lot of this information sounded eerily familiar. It's supposed to. This book was intended to ring a few bells and awaken a few sleeping dogs.

Perhaps you've always had your reservations about a certain coworker, but you buried those concerns because you thought you were just being paranoid or overly sensitive. Or, maybe you've tolerated an insufferable relative for twenty years, while lacking the dialogue needed to discuss the relative in question with other family members. Now that you've read this book, you have the knowledge and the framework to help you organize your suspicions regarding certain people in your life.

You realize that there is validity to your feelings and that the bitch in Marketing is definitely a W3, and that Uncle Irving always has been and always will be a W4. Now you've got the dialog. And now you've got the affirmation that you were always seeking. You know what to call these people; you know what secrets they might be hiding; and you know how to spot any new Wackos who might cross your path. And, perhaps most importantly, you know that you aren't alone in your battles against Wackos.

Do not, under any circumstances, beat yourself up for being judgmental—that's one of those internal struggles that can really backfire. When we automatically accept unacceptable behavior because we don't want to judge others, the only thing we gain is another Wacko in our lives. Stop wearing your heart on your sleeve. Or, if you must, put on a jacket!

Stop wearing your heart on your sleeve. Or, if you must, put on a jacket!

This book was meant to make you think about the people you share your life with and assess the qualities of those people. You will discover there are people you are definitely better off without; you will also gain an entirely new appreciation for the people in your life who are your truest supporters and friends.

By all means, judge a person. Judge his character. Judge his integrity. And then decide if he's worth your time.

Life is too short to live it with Wackos. So use what you've learned in this book to test the sincerity of the people in your life, and stop giving the wrong people the shirt off your back. There's no need to memorize the Wacko levels and traits. You can turn to this book time and again for validation when your instincts are warning you to make a fast getaway.

Now, let's review the characteristics of the host personality and each of the four Wacko levels.

The Host is the Most Vulnerable

While each and every person is susceptible to the negative effects of the Wackos in the world, it is those with "host" personalities who are the most vulnerable. Hosts are more likely to tolerate Wackos for longer intervals, and thus they leave themselves exposed to heavier doses of Wacko behavior.

A host, in fact, may inadvertently attract Wackos because her Mother Teresa Syndrome makes her an easy target. This syndrome is composed of the need to be loved and accepted by everyone and to please all others at virtually any cost. A host's other traits typically include a fear of standing in her personal power, an unnatural eagerness to "laugh off" almost any criticism, a penchant to apologize profusely and an inability to handle compliments.

Wackos will try their hardest to exploit these host qualities in their attempts to make hosts appear weak and foolish. Maureen did everything she could to make me feel clueless, when, in fact, she was the one who was. Selflessness does not equal brainlessness. Kindness does not equal weakness.

Sometimes being a host is like being a deer in hunting season. Everyone wants to take a shot at you. That is why when I reached my forties I stopped talking, and I started really listening to what comes out of other people's mouths. When I isolated those people who just wanted to use me for target practice, I cleaned house.

Hosts are highly susceptible to having Wacko experiences because their personalities dictate that they open their hearts and arms to virtually everyone around them. This doesn't mean that non-hosts are immune to Wackos. It just means that hosts need to pay closer attention to the Wacko traits and do a more thorough job of analyzing their current relationships and new acquaintances. Whether or not the host label is a perfect fit for you, you still may be susceptible to the negative influences of Wackos; after all, the higher levels are cunning and clever enough to strike when our defenses are down, and they cover their tracks. Non-hosts must also pay close attention to the Wacko traits but will probably have an easier time booting Wackos from their lives.

Sometimes being a host is like being a deer in hunting season. Everyone wants to take a shot at you.

What Were Those Wacko Traits Again?

There are four ascending Wacko levels—each more bizarre than the previous one. Like interest on a savings account that compounds daily, Wacko behavior will steadily build upon itself and is, for the most part, cumulative, meaning Wacko traits developed in Level 1 will typically still be present in a Wacko who ascends to Level 4.

Wackos themselves also suffer because of their behavior. Wackos typically have health problems, they have difficulty severing their mothers' apron strings, and they will begin to lose friends at a rapid rate as their behavior branches out into the upper levels. In fact, W3s seem to follow a carefully scripted pattern designed to drive friends away. W4s are simply so self-loving that they don't even desire "real" friends. They simply choose to surround themselves with pawns for their twisted little games.

Does a Wacko need to fit neatly into one particular category? Absolutely not. It's not uncommon for a Wacko to seesaw between levels as he or she tests and hones new traits. (Think Genevieve's mother-in-law, Wanda.) The best way to accurately categorize a Wacko is to focus on their most dominant Wacko traits—the ones most often exhibited—and make your designation from there.

Wacko 1

The lowest Wacko level often begins to appear during adolescence in the form of intense sibling rivalry. The examples we discussed included an older brother, Michael, who constantly belittled and berated his younger brother, Steven; and Sarah, who wouldn't show a smidgeon of affection toward her younger sister, Suzanne. We also met an adult who was the quintessential W1: Genevieve's mother-in-law, Wanda. W1s disparage and destroy others as a means of camouflaging their own insecurities.

Wacko 1 traits to watch for include:

I Do No Wrong
I'm a Tattletale
I Brandish a Sharp Tongue
I have Difficulty Giving Affection
I'm Antisocial

Wacko 2

W2s are the awkward, insecure middle-schoolers of Wacko-hood. These types are wedged between young W1s, who are excitedly learning to cultivate and wield their Wacko traits, and the higher levels of Wackos who are confident and skilled. W2s waffle between being normally functioning human beings and crazed lunatics. The prime example of a W2 that we discussed was Debra, the wife of one of Ched's good friends. Time spent with Debra was like time spent with two completely different personalities.

Look for these traits in a Wacko 2:

Who Am I Now? Dr. Jekyll or Mr. Hyde?
Watch Out for My "Look"
I'm Paranoid
I'm Never Wrong—Ever!
I'm Obsessive
The Best Offense is a Great Defense Mechanism

Wacko 3

The world that W3s live in is like no world that a host could ever know or understand. W3s are happy when (and only when) their lives are chaotic. For a W3, there can be no peace or serenity. There can be no status quo. There can only be turmoil, morning, noon and night. These same Wackos can bait their hooks and reel unsuspecting innocent ones into their Wacko world. My husband and I were completely fooled by a W3 named Coach Bully, and I somehow survived mountains of mayhem during a brief, but damaging, business affair with a W3 named Maureen.

To avoid suffering the same fate with a similar someone, watch out for these traits:

Pandemonium is My Drug
I Live on the Phone
I Am Self-Absorbed
I Am Emotionally Unstable
I Hold Grudges

Wacko 4

Wacko Level 4 is where most of the serious damage occurs. By the time a Wacko reaches this level, he has fine-tuned his Wacko traits to make them almost impossible to detect by others. These actors and actresses can fool virtually anyone— or at least anyone who hasn't read this book! The examples we discussed were my friend Sheila's ex-husband, Phil, who physically abused his wife but still successfully gained full custody of their children and managed to convince other townspeople that Sheila was the one with the problem; and Will, my friend Tina's former employer, who even had the IRS fooled.

The watch, look and listen technique isn't as effective with this type because of a W4's acting ability. After all, at least in the examples I gave, these people could be classified as criminals who managed to escape prosecution. However, if you can be impartial enough to spot the following traits, and if you give your instincts carte blanche, you can save yourself a lot of trouble.

Again, the Wacko 4 traits include:

It's All About Control
I Must Be the Center of Attention
It's All a Game
I'm Threatened by the Powerful
I'm Entitled to Pry

What Have We Learned?

If you remember anything at all about what you've read between these covers, remember these three things:

▶ How it begins is how it ends.

▶ You will never be the exception to how Wackos treat people.

▶ Watch, look and listen.

How it begins is how it ends is a phrase with infinite applications. It is an exceptionally useful motto when it comes to relationships with Wackos. Haven't we all had a failed relationship (or had a bad business experience), only to be rudely reminded by our own hindsight that red flags were waving wildly from the beginning? When that tiny voice inside you quietly opposes the way someone else is acting, you'd better listen closely. Very few relationships that begin on a sour note will go on to thrive harmoniously.

You will never be the exception to how Wackos treat people. This cannot be repeated enough. Hosts, in particular, seem to always give others the benefit of the doubt. It's OK to be gracious and cordial; that doesn't mean that every person you meet is a candidate for best-friend status. When you witness a Wacko mistreating another person, you can bet the Wacko will mistreat you in the same way. You will never be the exception—no matter how respectful you are, no matter how honest you are, no matter how understanding you are. Wackos are who they are. It doesn't matter who *you* are.

Watch, look and listen vigilantly and objectively. Watch the people who come and go from your life and look closely at how they treat others. Listen carefully to what people say about other people, and listen to your own instincts. This technique will help you spot the red flags early on. It sounds simple, but sometimes we see what we want to see and hear what we want to hear. Watch closely and listen honestly.

Y ou've got the information; now, what do you do with it? I've compiled a list of ten discussion questions to ask yourself or talk about with your spouse or a trusted friend if you've pinpointed a relationship that you feel needs further analysis. Try to come up with as many specific examples as you can for each question. Keep in mind that consistent, repeating behavior patterns should be cause for concern—not an occasional social slip-up or faux pas. Most people, for instance, have giddily engaged in sharing a particularly juicy morsel of gossip from time to time. This sporadic and benign scandal swapping is a far cry from the continuous mud slinging that Wackos thrive upon. You know the difference in your head and in your heart. Be completely open and honest with yourself when you consider the following questions:

▶ When I first met this person, was there anything tangible or intangible that raised a red flag in my mind?

▶ When this person exhibits kindness, do the actions seem sincere or do they seem rehearsed or forced?

▶ Does this person speak kindly about other people? Or does this person seem to derive pleasure from airing dirty laundry?

▶ When this person talks to me, is he/she interested in hearing how my day is going? Or would this person be just as happy conversing with a mirror?

- When I'm finished spending time with this person (or speaking with this person on the phone) do I feel refreshed and invigorated by our conversation, or do I feel deflated and exhausted by this person's emotional and psychological drama?

- Is our relationship based upon equality and even doses of give and take? Or, is one person predominantly giving and one person predominantly taking?

- Did I ever really *watch, look and listen* in regards to this person? Or, do I need to repeat these steps more thoroughly?

- After meeting this new person, would I feel safe sharing personal information with this person?

- Have I witnessed this person treating others in a way that makes me uneasy?

- Does this person seem truly interested in knowing and accepting the "real" me, or do they seem to have preconceived notions or a pre-written agenda that they want me to follow?

If, after considering the three principles in Chapter 20 and asking yourself these ten questions, you've uncovered a Wacko in your life, move on as quickly as you can. Don't waste your precious time trying to psychoanalyze or "save" the Wacko. My five-year-old, Chloe, says it best. When I ask her why the front of her shirt is wet, her response is "Because it is." Wackos are the way they are because that's the way they are. It is what it is. You can't change them, so move on.

I have my daughter, Paris, so well trained with her instincts that she will whisper in my ear, "Mommy, I don't like that person's energy."

Chapter 22 The Last Word

Different people will have different reactions to their Wacko experiences. Some people will emerge from the situation with renewed determination; some will emerge angry; others may emerge fearful of meeting new people and entering into new friendships. Others still may mourn the loss of a friendship that they once felt was valid.

All of these emotions are legitimate responses. My hope is that, after reading this book, you will realize how much better off you are without this person in your life. Your true friends are the ones deserving of your time and efforts.

How My Last Wacko Experience Changed My Life

After my last Wacko experience with Maureen, I felt like I'd been run over by a freight train. Once I picked up the remains of my shattered self-respect, I told myself I would never let anyone treat me badly again, and I meant it. When I observe Wacko characteristics in a new acquaintance, I pay close attention to them, and I don't hoodwink myself into believing "I can handle it." Yeah, maybe I can handle the Wackos out there *but* I choose not to. I am vigilant about whom I spend my time with and would prefer solitude over distress any day of the week. I have learned to love myself too much to be upset emotionally or physically by anyone.

An extreme example demonstrating how I've changed would be a recent trip to Mexico I took with my family. First, let me say that I'm convinced that in a past life I got lost somewhere and something dreadful happened to me. Every time I get lost, I lose it. Suffering from this phobia has been so embarrassing for me. I have literally had to train my children to pat my head and calmly reassure me that we will be fine whenever I happen to take a wrong turn in the car. Believe me; they do it every time I get lost. The only problem is that I didn't pass this calming technique on to my husband.

I have learned to love myself too much to be upset emotion-ally or physically by anyone.

So there we were vacationing in Mexico when we left a restaurant late one night. While driving back to the rental house, Ched took a wrong turn. Once you're off a main road in Mexico, you're almost guaranteed to get lost, unless you are some Wacko level I don't know about yet. I started breaking into a sweat as I begged Ched to turn around and go back the other way.

"I know where I am! Would you calm down?" he yelled at me. He was right; I needed to calm down, but the kids started to get nervous and I couldn't stop badgering Ched. I was petri-fied that we would be lost for hours.

Finally, Ched pulled the car over to the side of the road and told me to drive home. "If you are so sure I'm lost, you drive home," he said firmly and with immense disdain.

As we got out of the car to switch places, Ched came face to face with a Mexican police officer. Neither of us had noticed the parked police car just a few yards up the street from where we pulled over.

The officer questioned Ched and demanded to know if he were carrying any weapons. A week before our trip, my father-in-law had given Ched his combat knife from Vietnam. It is something Ched had looked forward to inheriting his whole life, and once he had it in his possession, he carried it with him virtually everywhere. As I stood by my car door watching them talk, I saw the officer's eyes narrow. Ched had come clean about having the knife with him—he thought honesty would be best in this situation. The officer clearly knew that the knife was valuable, and he wanted it. The two of them walked up to me, and the officer asked me in strained English if I was all right.

Ched leaned toward me and whispered, "Honey, if I give him the knife he will let us go."

I looked the officer square in the eyes and said firmly, "You are not getting that knife. That's was my husband's father's knife and you aren't getting it!"

"Christina, if I don't give him the knife he'll call back up," Ched whispered.

"Fine, let him call back up," I told Ched, making sure the officer understood I was on to him.

To make a long story short, we ended up at the police station, but I stood firm on my conviction that the knife belonged to Ched. "You are not getting that knife! That is my husband's knife, and you can't have it," I said with my arms across my chest like a five-year-old taking a stand.

Ched finally looked at the police chief and said, "What do you want to clear this up?"

"Fifty dollar," the corrupt chief said with a smile as wide as my size 8 ½ shoes are long.

I was done being pushed around. How had my last Wacko experience changed me? I had made up my mind to be the one in charge of my life.

My final example relates directly to how this book came to fruition. After writing the first draft of my manuscript, I started searching for an editor. I called a number in the phonebook and scheduled an appointment. I pulled into the driveway of the editor's office and was immediately turned off by the appearance of the building. The building just didn't say "success" to me.

Once I was inside, the editor proudly showed me the wall displaying all of the books he had helped edit. He had wall shelves lined with both hard covers and paperbacks. There was just one problem. A quick scan of the book covers and titles revealed five or six copies of each book, as if I were stupid enough not to notice that they were all the same.

The editor sat down behind his desk, and I warily took a seat across from him. My guard was up. My instincts were telling me to run. He reached across the table to take my manuscript from me, but I immediately pulled it to my chest. "You know what? I don't feel right about this," I said.

He immediately asked me if he had done something wrong.

"No, that's not it. I just don't feel right about this." We sat in awkward silence for a moment, and then I slowly rose from my seat. "I have to leave now," I said calmly. I knew I didn't need to explain myself or my decision to leave. I was polite and spoke my truth, and I trusted my instincts. I kept my sentences short and to the point. As I result, I found another editor who I instantly felt comfortable with, and you've just finished reading the results.